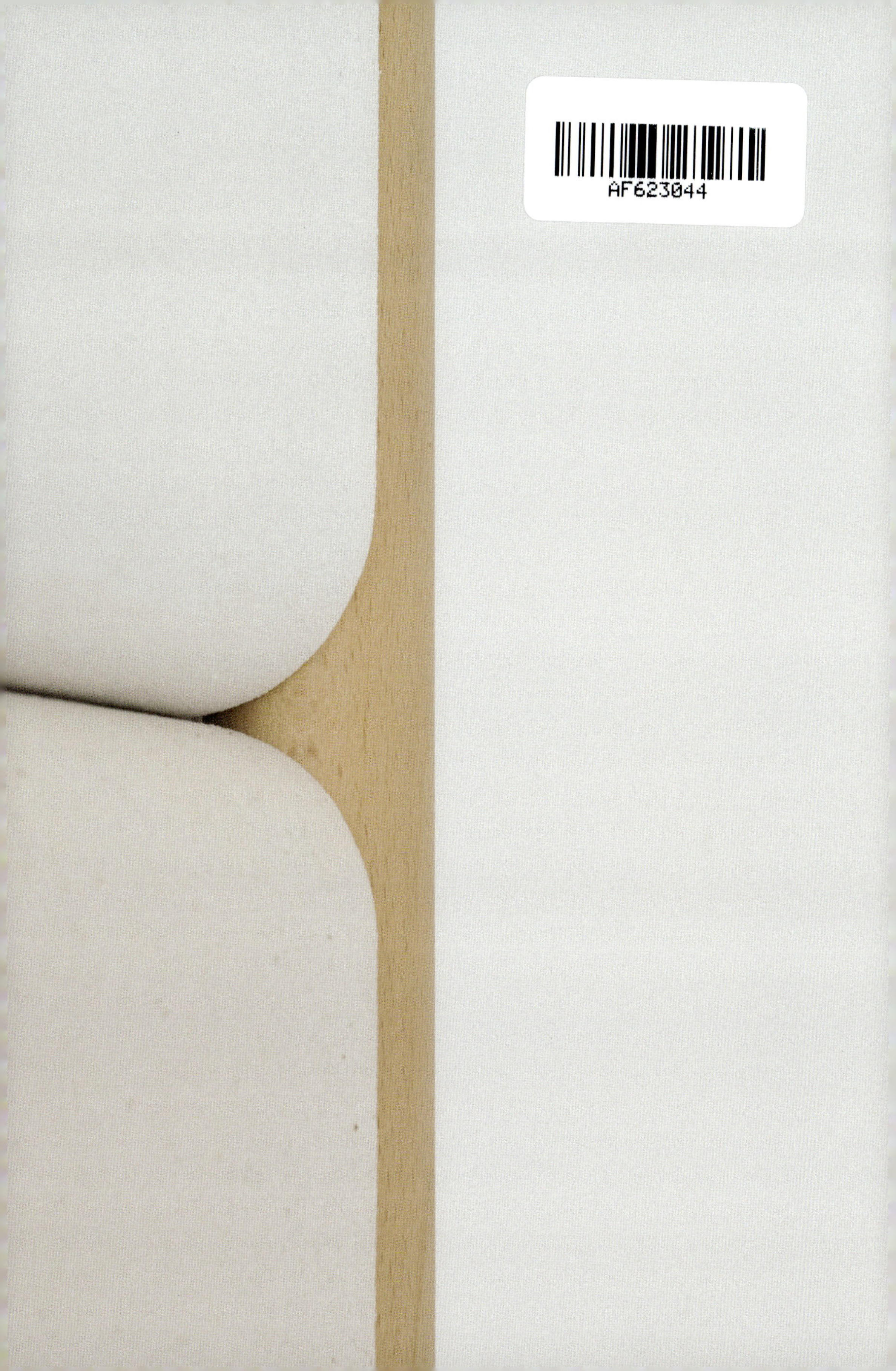

Fahd Burki
daydreams

Art Jameel Mousse Publishing

This book has been published by
Art Jameel and Mousse Publishing
in conjunction with the exhibition:

Fahd Burki
daydreams
Curated by Dawn Ross

Jameel Arts Centre
5 March – 9 October, 2022

Editors
Dawn Ross and Lucas Morin

Editorial Coordination
Lucas Morin (Art Jameel)

Publishing Editor
Antonio Scoccimarro
(Mousse Publishing)

Texts
Saira Ansari, Dawn Ross, Murtaza Vali

Copy Editing
Muriel Kahwagi, Lindsey Westbrook

Graphic Design
Dina Al Khatib (Art Jameel)

Special thanks to
Rhoda Azizoghly, Umer Butt,
Fady Jameel, Albert Kolambel,
Elaine Lubguban and Hetal Pawani

Published and distributed by
Art Jameel
Jameel Arts Centre
Jaddaf Waterfront
Dubai, United Arab Emirates
artjameel.org

Mousse Publishing
Via Pier Candido Decembrio 28
20137, Milan, Italy
moussemagazine.it

Available through
Mousse Publishing, Milan
moussepublishing.com

DAP | Distributed Art Publishers,
New York
artbook.com

Idea Books, Amsterdam
ideabooks.nl

Les presses du réel, Dijon
lespressesdureel.com

First edition: 2022

Printed in Italy by Tipografia
Valdostana, Aosta

ISBN 978-8-86-749621-1

€27 Euros / $30 US Dollars

Unless otherwise noted, all images are courtesy of the artist and Grey Noise, Dubai, and photographed by Shahzeb Bhatti.

Inside cover (front): *Minutes before I fall asleep* (detail), 2019, wood, canvas, acrylic paint, 100.2 × 77 × 4.2 cm. Photo by Umar Nadeem.

Image pp. 6-7: Fahd Burki's studio, Lahore, 2020. Photo by Umar Nadeem.
Images pp. 44-45 are courtesy of Art Jameel. Photos by Ismail Noor.
Images pp. 109-123 and inside cover (back) are courtesy of Art Jameel. Photos by Daniella Baptista.

Mr Abdelmonem bin Eisa Alserkal Collection, pp. 65, 66
Rahil Anwar Collection, p. 15
Collection of the Art Gallery of New South Wales, p. 62
Art Jameel Collection, pp. 35, 68, 69, 80, 85, 105
Naazish Ata-Ullah Collection, p. 38
Juan Barros Collection, Lisbon, p. 64 (top)
Franck Barthelemy Collection, p. 54
China Belgravia Collection, p. 14
Farrukh Burki Collection, p. 39
Jean-Marc Decrop Collection, pp. 20, 23 (bottom right), 37
Julian & Stephanie Grose Collection, Adelaide, pp. 18, 72
Jones Family Collection, London, p. 73 (top)
Vilma Jurkute Collection, p. 89
Khurram Kasim Collection, pp. 19, 25, 78 (left), 84
Preena Khan Collection, p. 28
Payal and Anurag Khanna Collection, pp. 50, 59, 60, 63, 64 (bottom), 86, 102
Sage Mehta and Michael Robinson Collection, p. 88
Hetal Pawani Collection, p. 40 (bottom)
Preeti Pawani Collection, p. 55
Naresh Ponappa Collection, p. 57
Private Collection, p. 40 (top), 61
Prateek & Priyanka Raja Collection, Kolkata, p. 67
Rima Shazad Bokhari Collection, p. 42
Nagy Zard Collection, p. 78 (right)

ART JAMEEL

CONTENTS

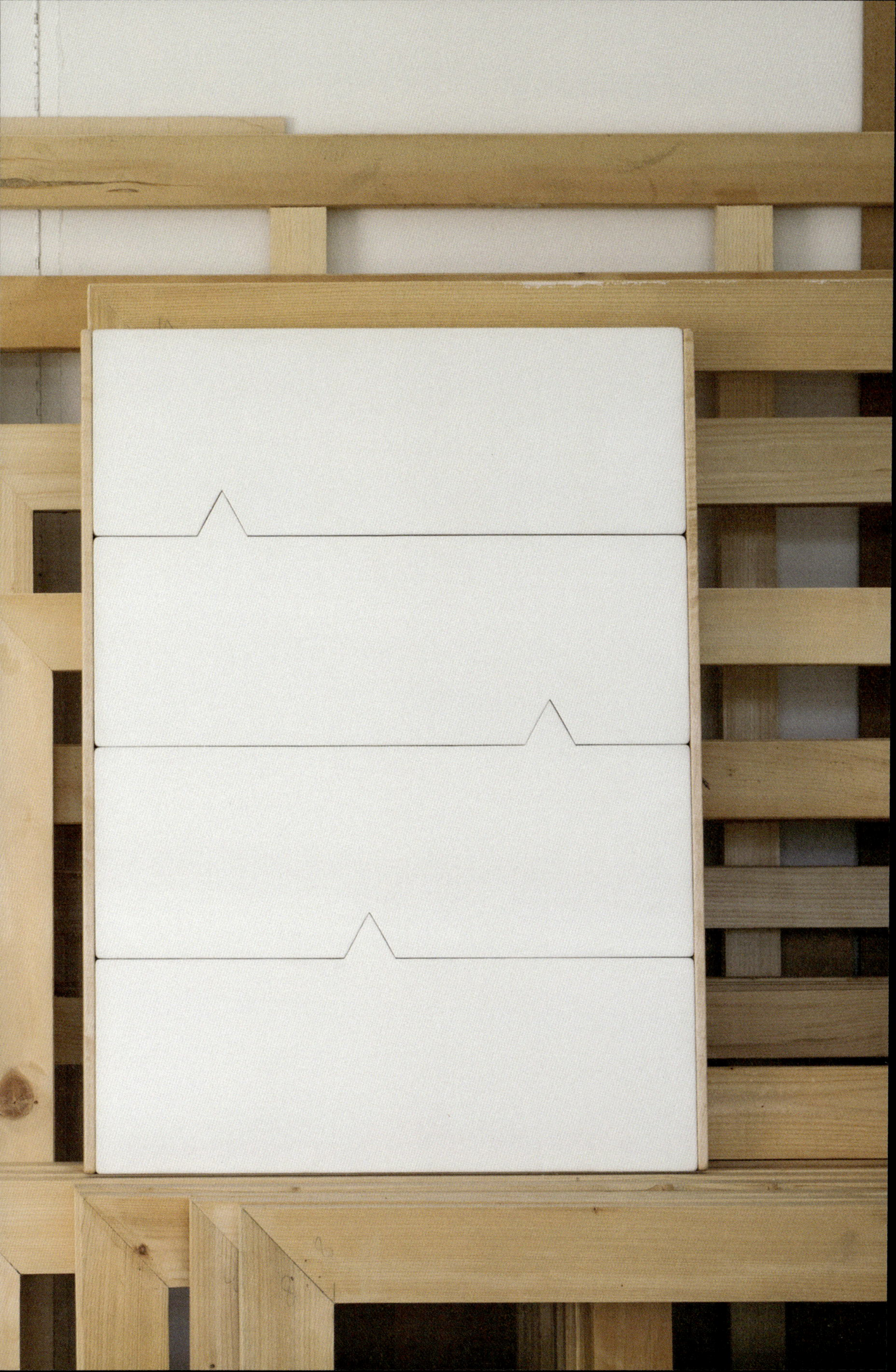

FOREWORD

Antonia Carver and Dawn Ross

This book was published on the occasion of Fahd Burki's first survey exhibition, *daydreams*, held at Jameel Arts Centre, Dubai, which brought together works spanning the previous fifteen years of the artist's practice. Art Jameel has had a long association with Fahd Burki, a relationship between institution and artist that is rooted as much in conversation and ideas as it is in the collecting and exhibiting of works. The year 2022 proved a timely moment for a solo show that opened up Fahd's highly considered sensibility and depth of studio practice to the Jameel's local and international audiences. *daydreams* was a tightly edited display of the artist's oeuvre – the selection of which was no mean feat, given the breadth and diversity of his body of work. The exhibition, and now, this book, has revealed a complex journey through concept, process, shape, colour, texture and technique.

Going beyond the function and character of an exhibition catalogue, this publication takes a personal look at Fahd's earlier life and work, and the evolution of his practice to date, enhancing our understanding of his larger oeuvre.

This monograph includes deeply studied, compelling and complementary essays by two eminent writers, Saira Ansari and Murtaza Vali. The contributors chronicle Fahd's influences, methods and approaches to making, and his extensive practice which ranges in scope from figuration to minimalist abstraction.

We are most grateful to the myriad lenders to the exhibition, both private and public, whose works have added so significantly to the broader scholarship and understanding of Fahd's work. We also acknowledge the huge contribution that Fahd's long-term collaborator and gallerist Umer Butt has made towards the realisation of this important project in all its facets.

The process of making this exhibition and book has been a true curatorial, scenographic and editorial partnership with the artist. Fahd's approach is meticulously deliberate yet open and generous; he continually pushes forward the boundaries and thought processes of both his own practice and that of his collaborators – including Art Jameel.

Antonia Carver, Director
Dawn Ross, Head of Collections
Art Jameel

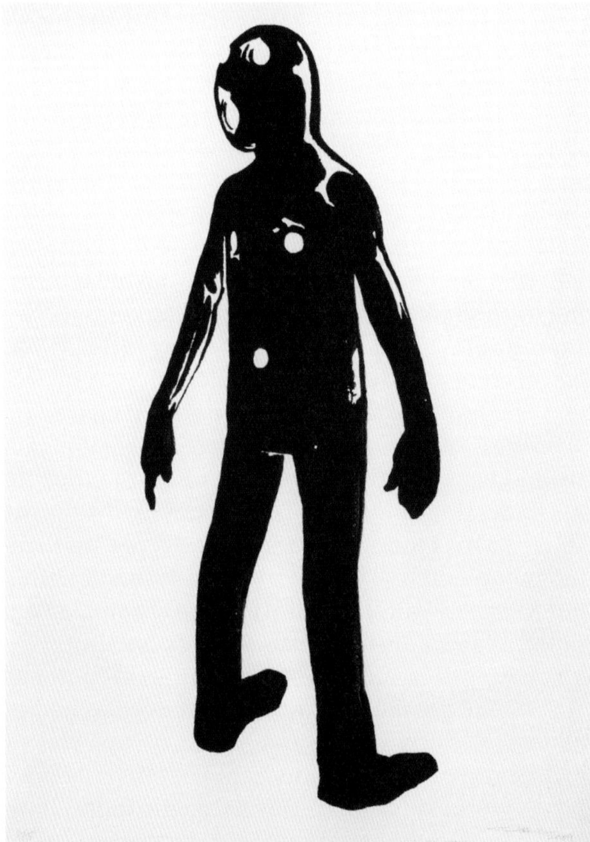

Untitled, 2009, screen print on paper, 91 × 66 cm

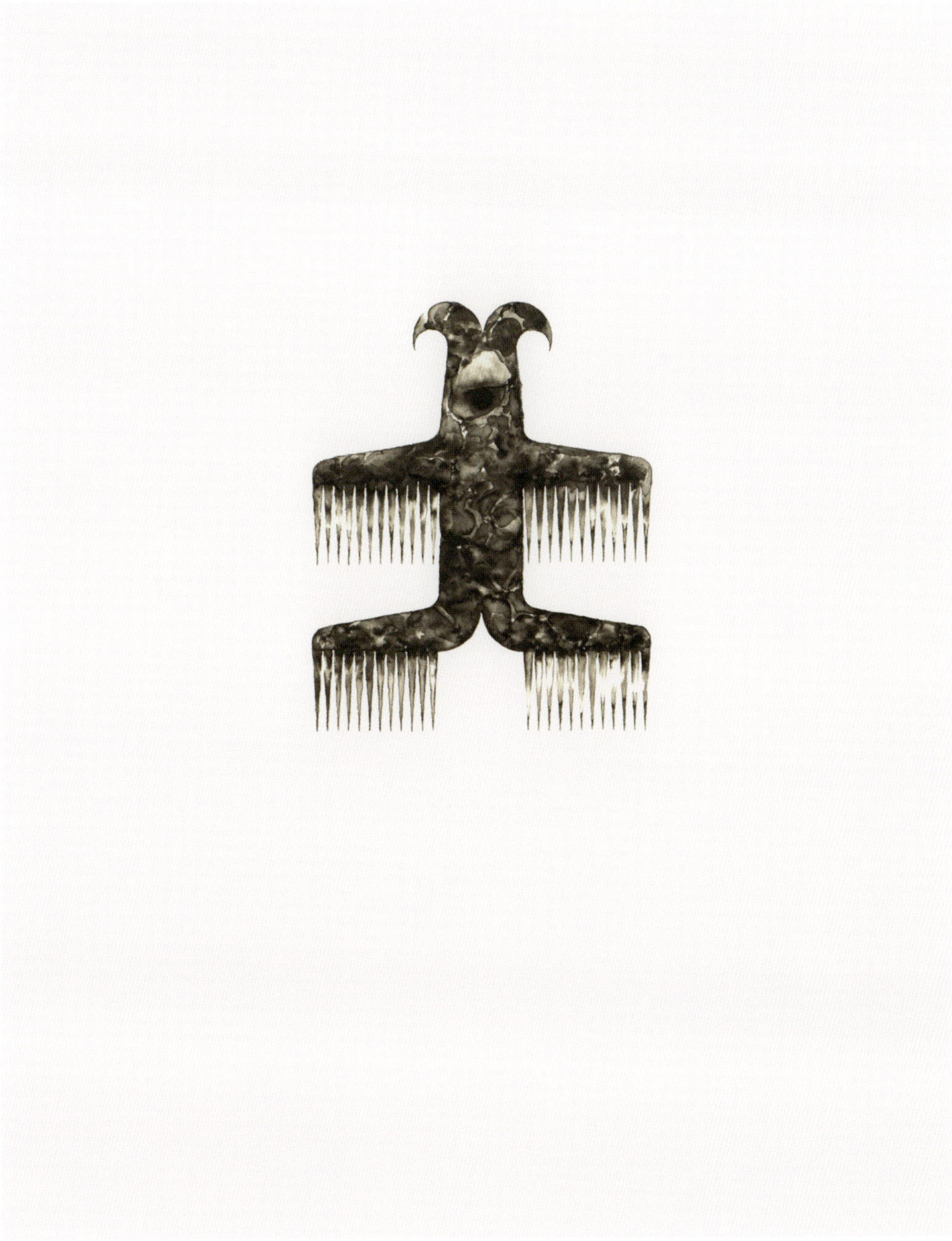

Malediction, 2009, Indian ink on paper, 152 × 122 cm

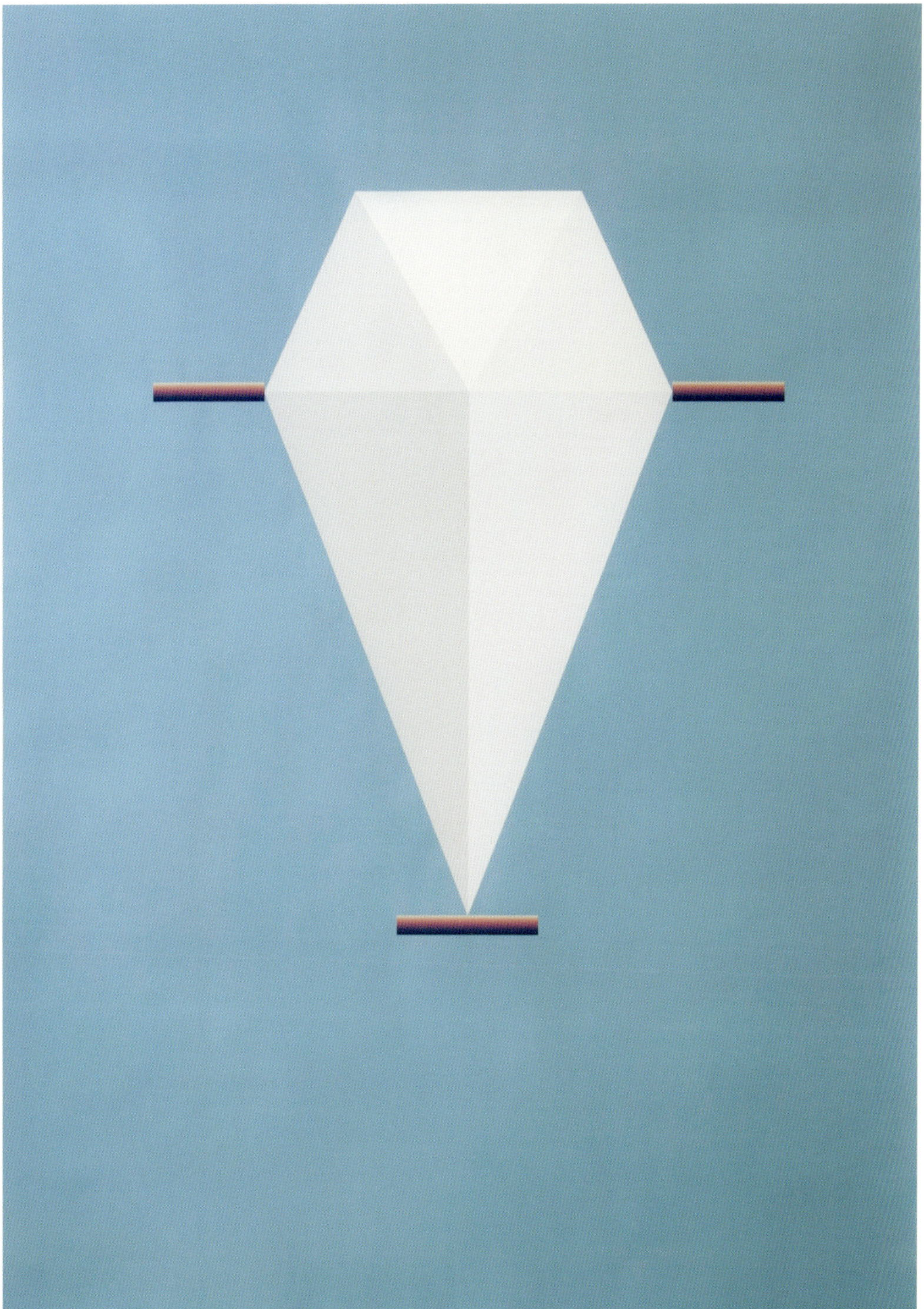

Untitled, 2012, acrylics and collage on paper, 218.44 × 138.7 cm

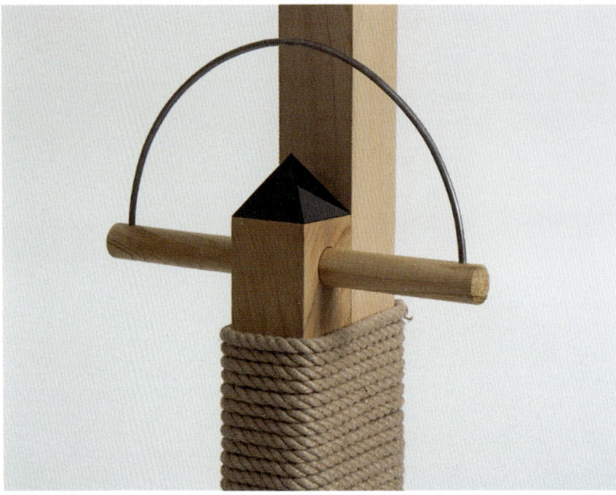

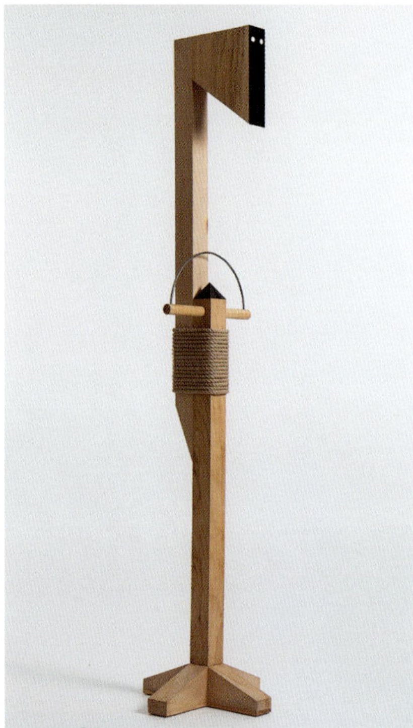

Liar, 2012, perspex, cedar, wood, rope and iron, 201.2 × 45.5 × 45.5 cm

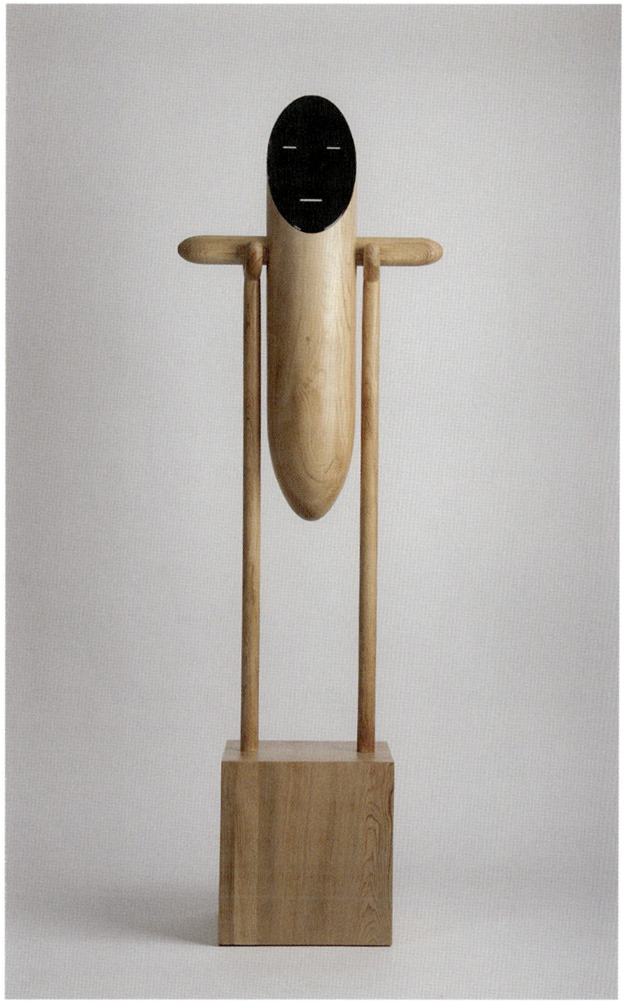

Optimist, 2012, perspex, cedar, 159 × 52 × 32.9 cm

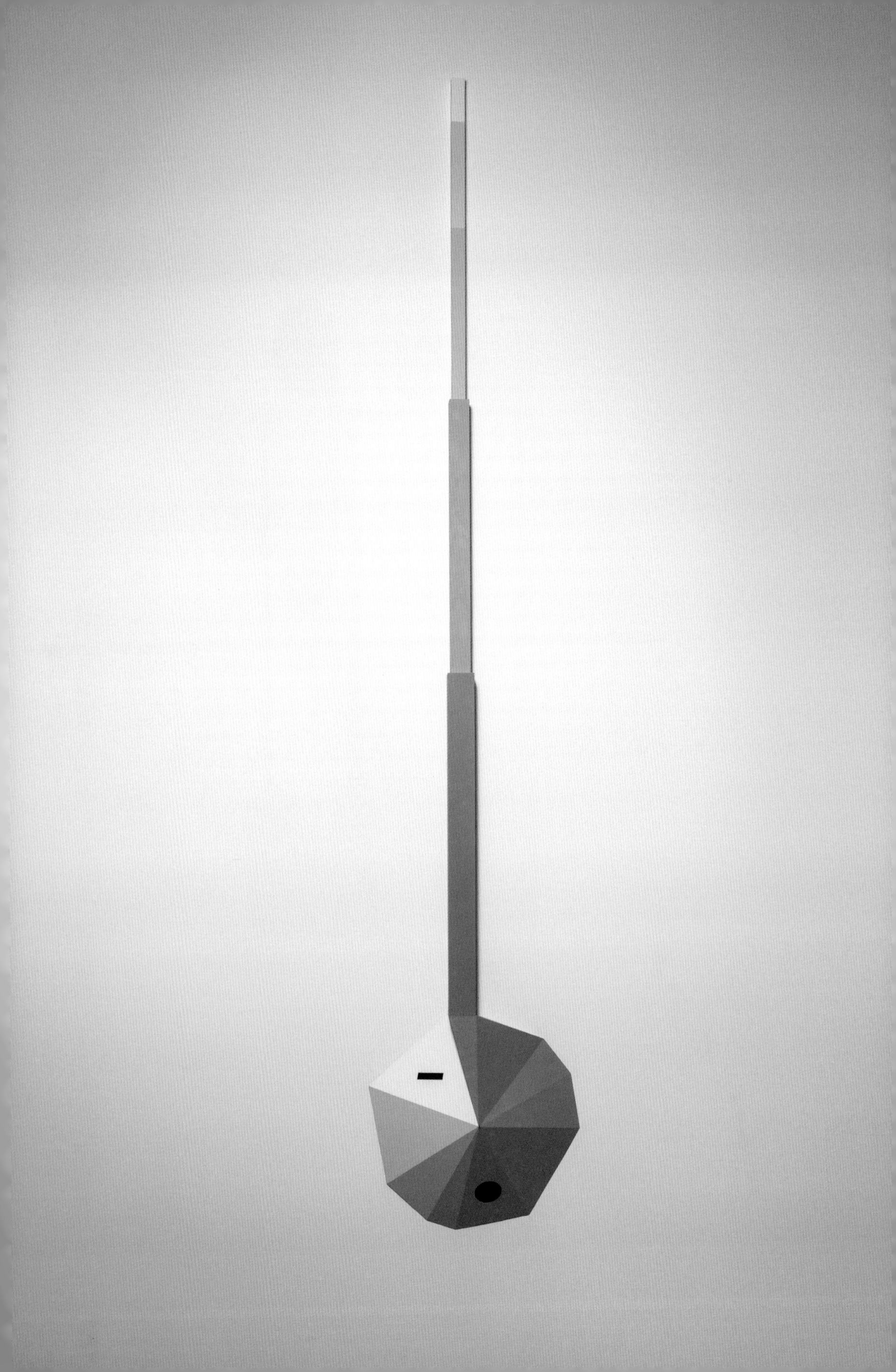

Interdimensional Mask, 2014, acrylic gesso on wood, 223.5 × 39.15 × 13 cm

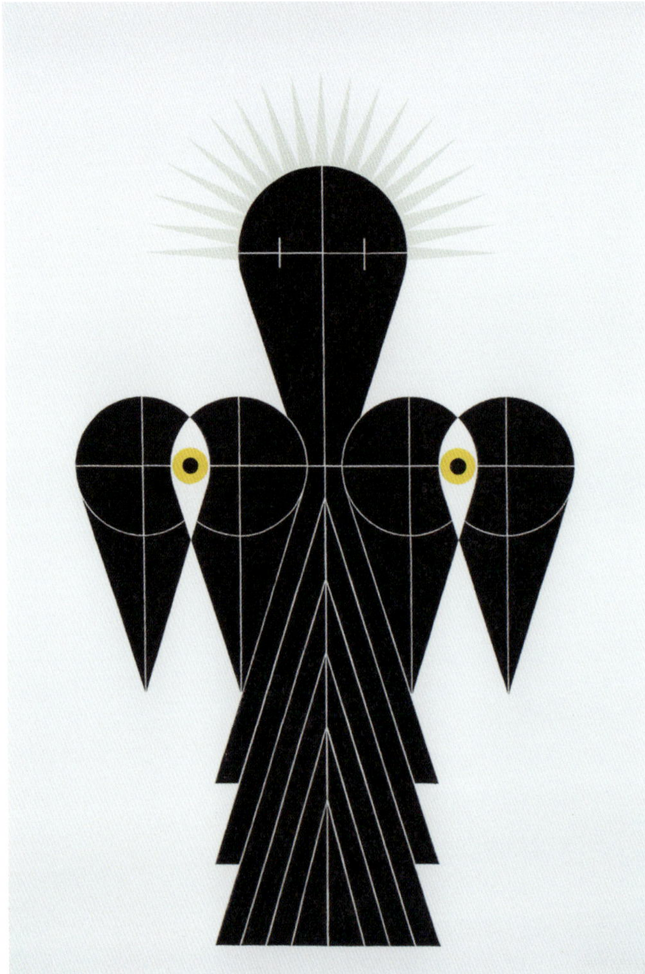

Saint Eclipse, 2012, acrylics on paper, 56 × 38 cm

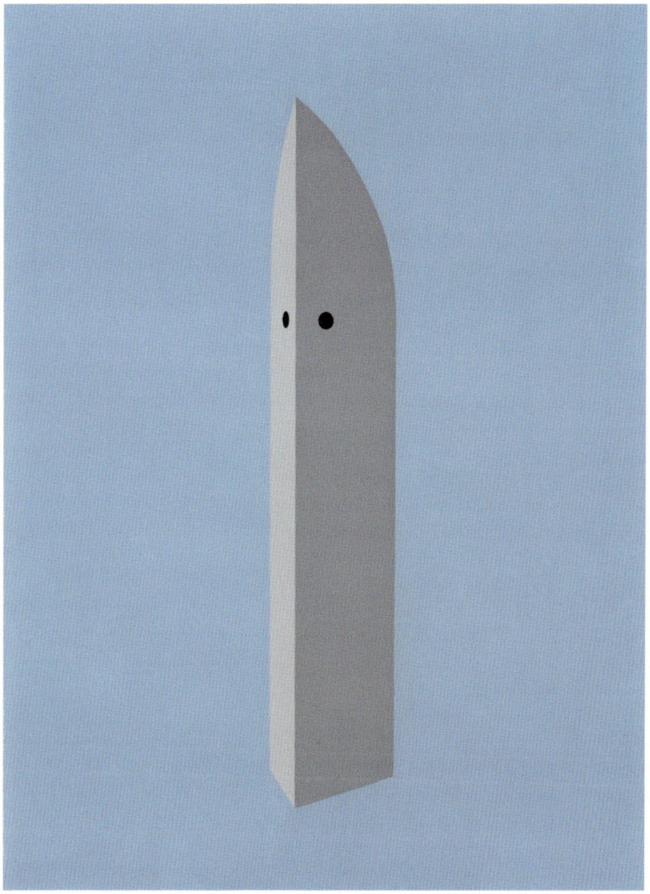

The Shape of Punishment, 2012, acrylics on paper, 51.2 × 38 cm

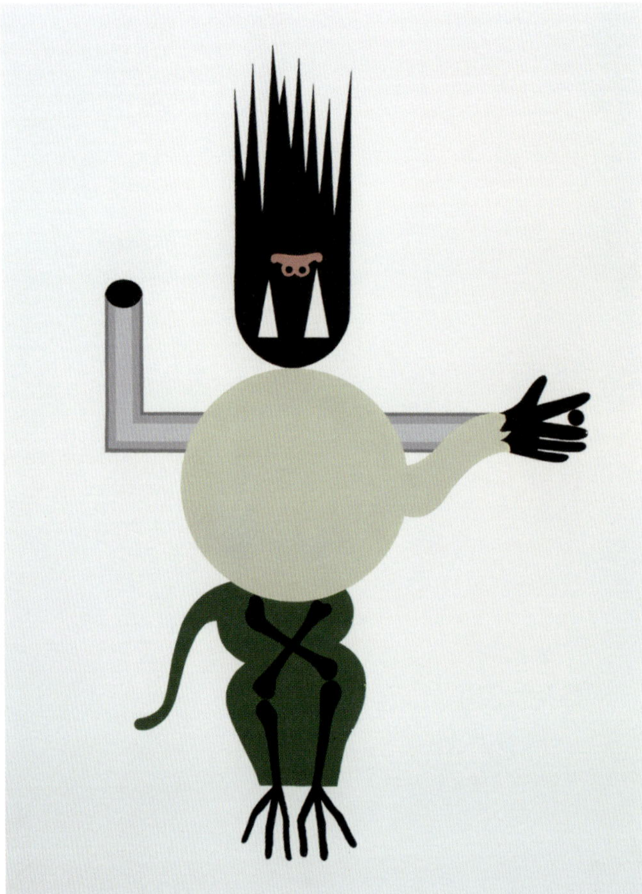

Bad Magic, 2012, acrylics on paper, 51 × 37.7 cm

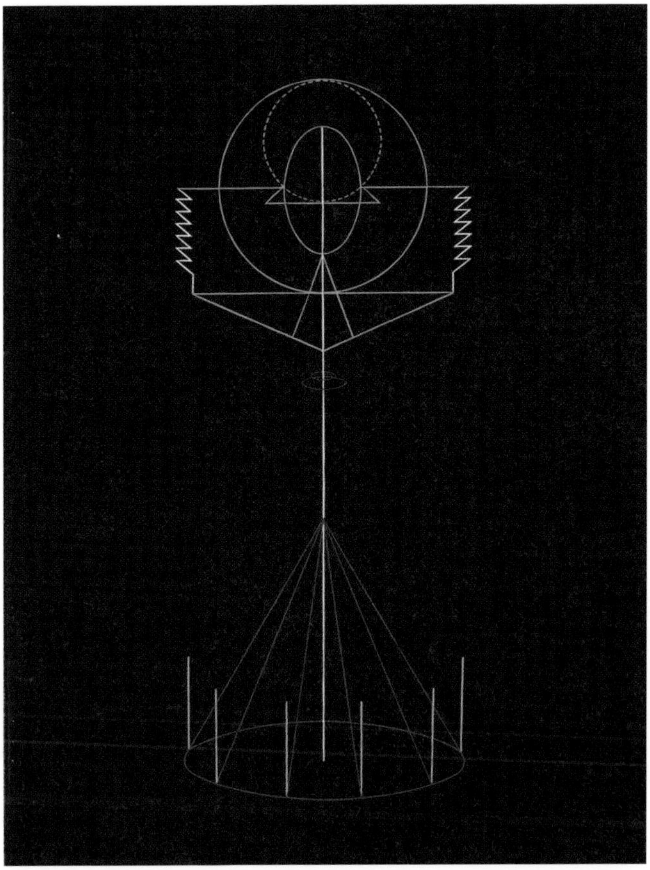

Prayer for Circuits, 2012, acrylics and marker on paper, 57 × 43.2 cm

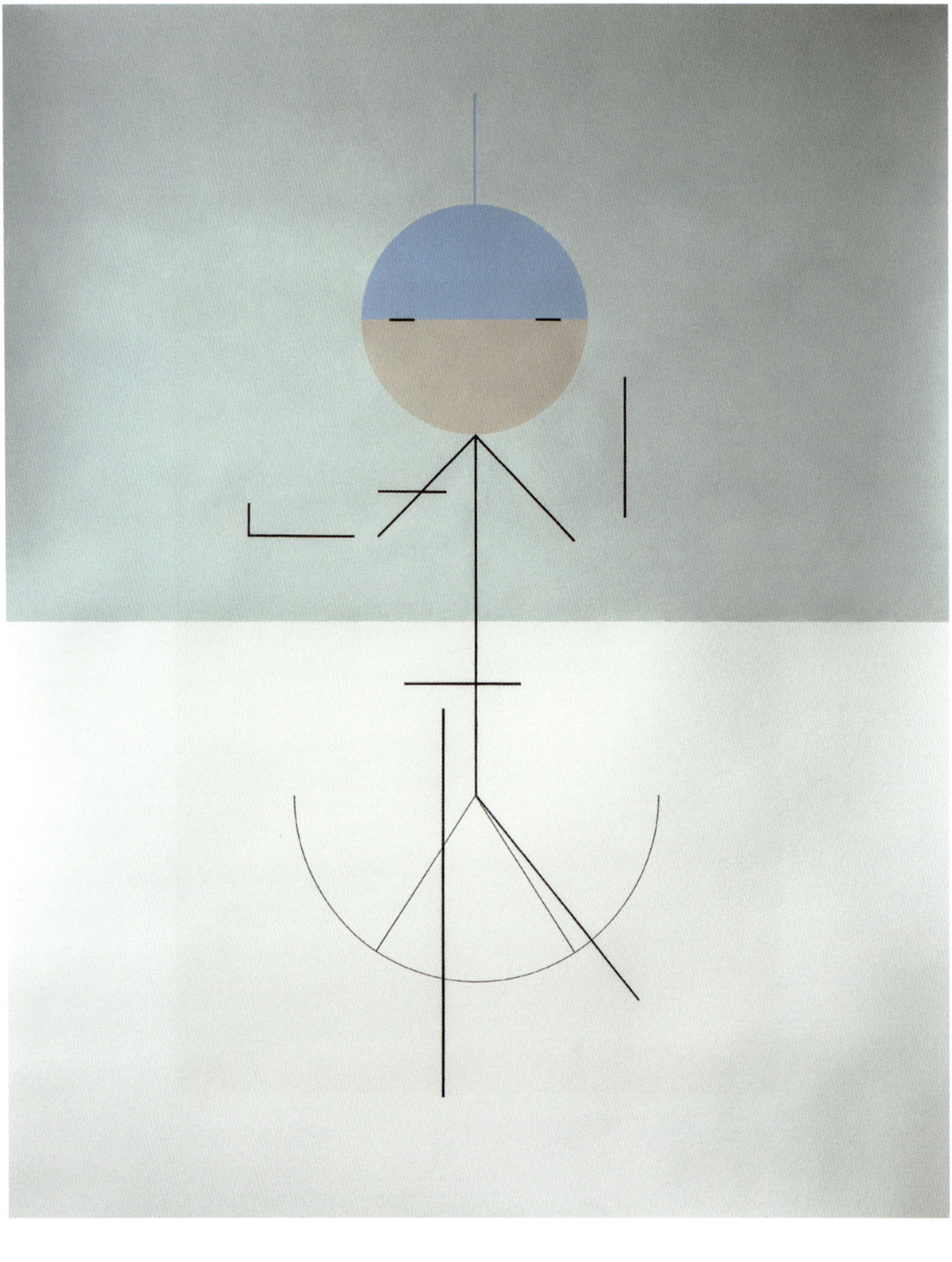

Bliss, 2014, acrylics and pen on paper, 152 × 122 cm

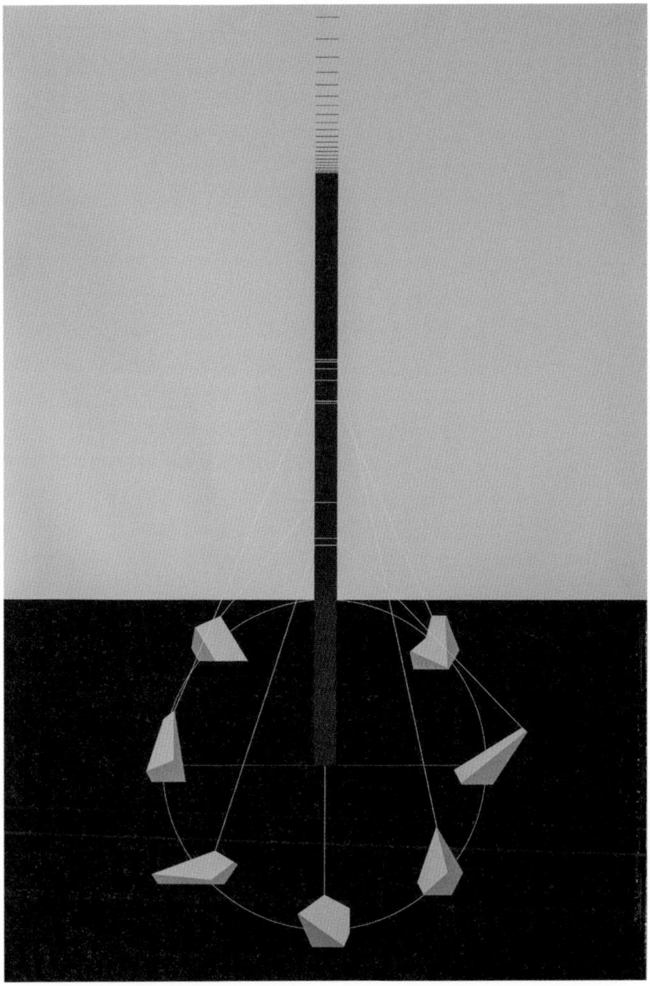

Ancestor's Circle, 2013, screen print on paper, 112.5 × 76.5 cm

Seeking Eden, 2014, charcoal and pastel pencil on paper, 154 × 101.3 cm

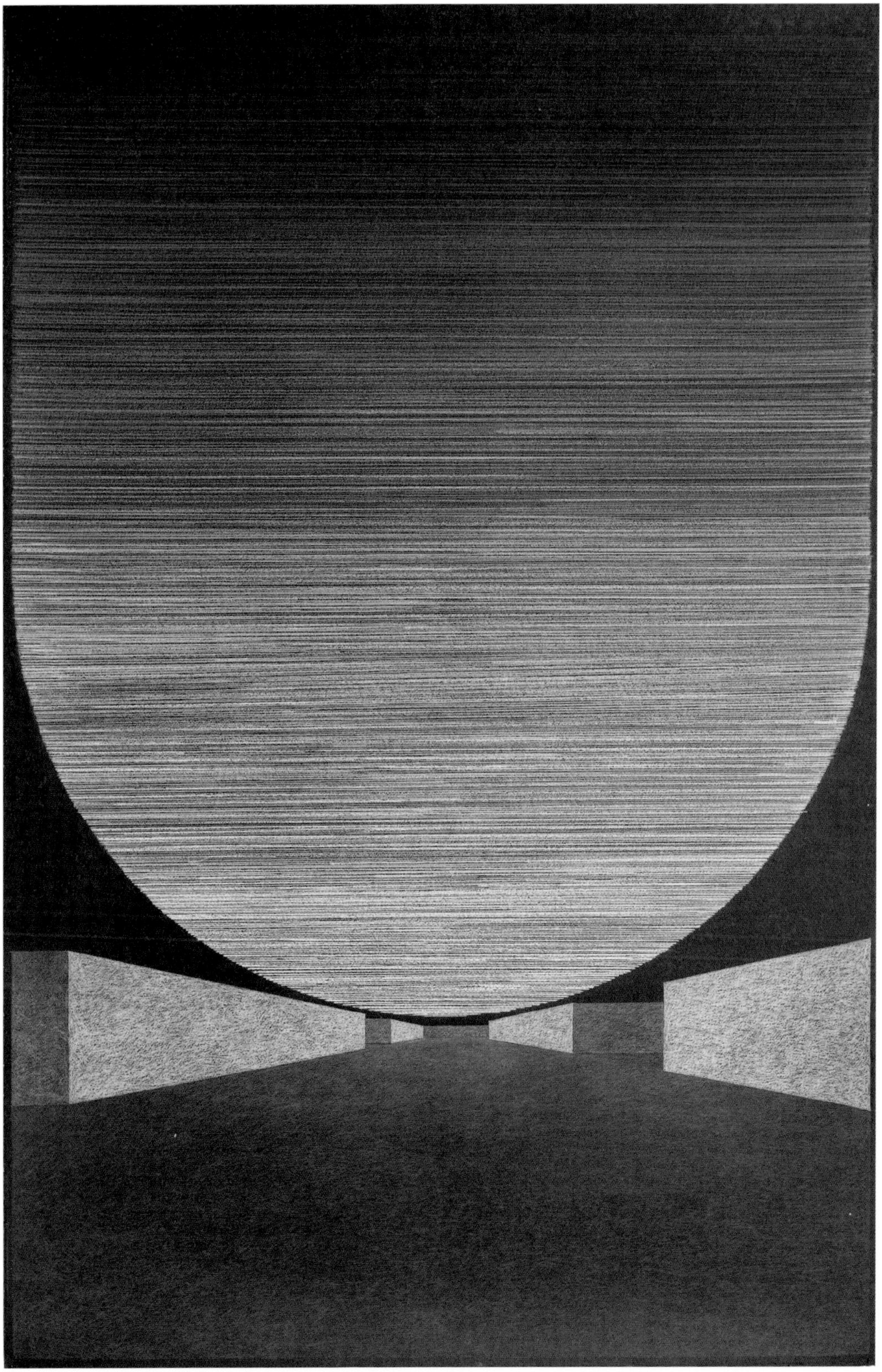

BORROWED MONSTERS

Popular Culture and Worldbuilding in the Works of Fahd Burki

Saira Ansari

The opening credits of Stanley Kubrick's film, *2001: A Space Odyssey,*[1] (1968) unfurl to the heroic fanfare of Richard Strauss's tone poem 'Also sprach Zarathustra' (1896) as the Sun rises over the Earth and Moon, creating circular shapes of blinding light and utter darkness. The silence afterwards transports us away from the celestial, and down to Earth where the 'Dawn of Man' plays out in a vast, sepia-tinted rock and desert landscape. The long and meticulous sequence is deliberately slow, building up to a synchronous climax with György Ligeti's cacophonic choral and orchestral symphony *Requiem* (1963–1965), as we see the cognitive capacity of man's anthropoid ancestors expanding after contact with a large and unworldly monolith that appears suddenly, as if from nowhere. Tall, rectangular, and dark, it is not of that land, nor of that time. Yet, it manipulates one of the creatures to wield a bone as a weapon so as to assume power and control of its destiny through an act of measured violence.

Much has been written about the film – the screenplay for which was co-written by Kubrick and science fiction writer Arthur C. Clarke[2] – its musical score, and the various interpretations of its beginning and end. The synthesis of these visuals and sounds have become so intrinsically bound to the storyline that they have become impossible to separate. Fahd Burki tells me he was greatly moved by Kubrick's creation and that the film left a lasting impact on his work. In particular, what stayed with him was the notion of scale – visualised not only through the sweeping views of land and vastness of open space, but also through the panoramic musical score which stretched and enveloped a range of human emotions.

1

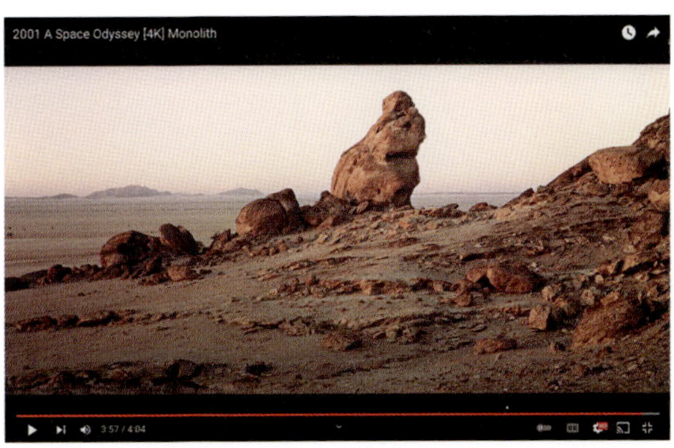

[2] The novel *2001: A Space Odyssey* was developed jointly by Arthur C. Clarke and Stanley Kubrick alongside the film version and published in 1968, soon after the release of the film. While Clarke and Kubrick both worked on the book, it is slightly different and more expansive than the film, and only Clarke is cited as the official author.

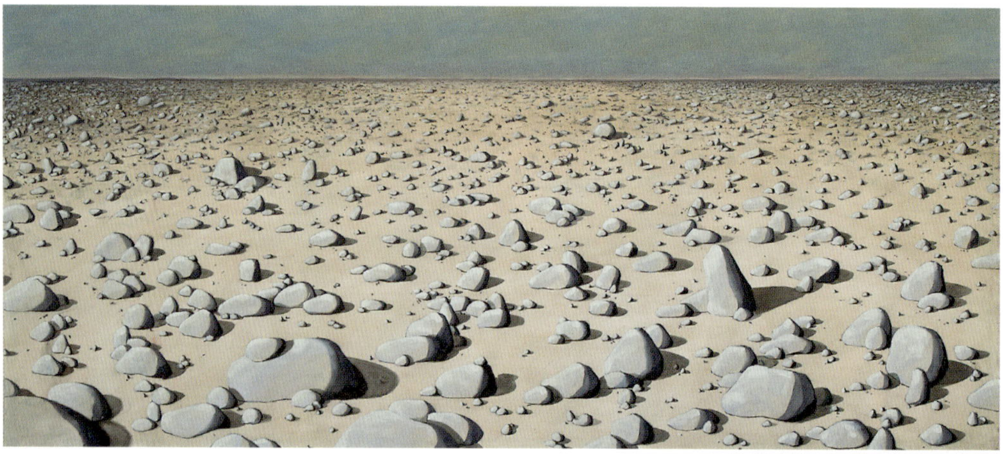

Tract I, 2006, oil on canvas, 168 × 366 cm

As I speak to Burki about the film, I revisit the desolate and stony landscape of *Tract I*, 2006, [p. 28] which was inspired in part by Kubrick's vision, and I suddenly have new insight into the artist's work that I had only guessed at before.

Fahd Burki and I both grew up in Lahore, Pakistan, and while we led significantly different lives, it seems that the smallness of Lahore ensured we shared similar coming-of-age experiences when the country was at the precipice of joining a globalised world. In the time before satellite television and cable networks, we turned to readily available mainstream English literature, including fantasy and science fiction novels and comic books. But another kind of change came swiftly after the death of military dictator General Muhammad Zia-ul-Haq in 1988. As the first private television channels started broadcasting in 1990 and dish antennas (satellite TV) proliferated in the mid-1990s, our generation became ardent consumers of imported popular culture that took over our television sets and bookshops. Meanwhile, bootlegged copies of rock and grunge music were being sold across town, which led to the development of a rich indie music scene, permeating both Burki's life and mine. So, it is no coincidence that many of the cultural references that those of us growing up in the urban centres of Pakistan adopted were external, alien even, yet they formed an intrinsic part of our spoken and visual vocabulary. Early MTV culture of cool, Hollywood blockbusters, post-war sci-fi, Japanese anime, and more; the influences were as varied as they were compelling. Very little of this material was in Urdu.

For too long, we have tried to find the right vocabulary for the rest of the world (as well as for purists back home) to understand how our practices – Burki's art and my writing – are Pakistani even when they don't look or sound it. In some ways, we may not fit the bill at all, and we are entirely comfortable with that; but in many other ways, we are the quintessential generation of city kids who grew up in the middle of an independent media revolution and, later, the arrival of the Internet.

Burki joined the National College of Arts Lahore (NCA) in 2000, and a year later, so did I. We both enrolled in the fine arts department and majored in painting. NCA was the first platform where we came face to face with peers from every province in the country, and where we encountered multiple regional languages and a diversity in heritage and skill sets to which we had not previously been exposed. NCA was both exciting and daunting, and the possibilities seemed infinite. Only in retrospect, and after much reflection, has it become possible to understand how the privileges and handicaps of our urban-hybrid cultural experiences shaped the way we navigated this period.

NCA is considered the premier art school of Pakistan and has been an authority in shaping artistic practices and market trends. It was originally established by the British Crown in 1875 as the Mayo School of Industrial Arts to train local craftsmen and galvanise the production of export-quality crafts. Although the college had significantly evolved since, remnants of the original curricula still lingered in our studios and theory classes in the early 2000s. Despite it being a progressive environment unparalleled by any other in the country, and claiming to be home to the free-spirited, we were often pegged down with moralistic weights that were difficult to dismiss. For students like me, there were multiple reminders in studio classes that we were relying on *borrowed* or *imposed* culture, and that to be truly authentic we must embrace what our heritage had to offer us. However, through those same channels, we were being taught history and technique with decidedly Western specifications and with terminology that existed only in English. It seemed, then, that Western content wasn't the problem. Instead, it was the yet-unresolved contemporary influences that the college struggled to locate within serious practice.

By his own account, Burki isn't much of a reader, but from an early age, he was consumed by the world of comics and graphic novels which laid the groundwork for his interest in drawing, illustration, and visual arts. Citing everything from cult-favourite Japanese animation *Akira* (1988) to the much-venerated collaborations between Mœbius (French cartoonist Jean Giraud) and Chilean-French filmmaker Alejandro Jodorowsky, Burki betrays an immense admiration for hand-drawn animation. In high school, he became friends with Murad Khan Mumtaz, now an established miniature painter and academic, who belongs to a family that is deeply entrenched in employing holistic and philosophical tenets to explore modernity and tradition; specifically, in the case of his father, Kamil Khan Mumtaz, in Islamic art and architecture. Conversations with Mumtaz had a profound effect on Burki and he decided to enrol at the NCA to study contemporary art. He would be the first in his family to do so.

While Burki was not interested in pursuing a practice of miniature painting, as Mumtaz was doing, he was deeply fascinated by its tradition, illustrative quality and form; the historical homogenising and bastardisation of it during colonial rule; and the continued self-fetishisation practised by artists decades later. He wondered why popular culture didn't seep into the traditional arts and why local folklore and stories weren't being adopted into art school coursework, or why formal manuscripts weren't being rendered in comic book format.

Once he had joined the NCA, many of Burki's 'non-fine-art' concerns were dismissed because the discourse did not have space for non-Pakistani pop culture. He found solace in a small group of students who shared with him common interests in film, anime, comics, and multiplayer fantasy videogames. But none of them were enrolled in the painting department. Unable to reconcile these two worlds – the sacred and the profane – he continued to operate in involuntary duality throughout the BFA programme. A year my senior, Burki's painting studio was a floor above mine and I remember vividly his thesis work from 2003: large, figurative, photorealistic oil paintings on canvas. There were hushed whispers among the students about Burki having developed a way to paint super-realistic-looking flesh and a grid-based system to scale photographic images at will, which seemed magical to those of us who had read – only in black-and-white photocopied books – about Rembrandt's technique for painting luminescent skin. Almost two decades later, Burki recalls that within the department, skill-based painting was considered the benchmark, the ideal to which he and his peers thought they ought to aspire.

Despite gravitating towards a certain version of academic painting and figurative art, Burki credits the guidance of two teachers, Nazish Ataullah and Maryam Hussein, for pushing him to dig deeper. He remembers how Hussein introduced him to works by painters such as Paula Rego, Lucian Freud, and Jenny Saville, among others, as a way of relooking at the body and understanding what it meant to paint it; a way to look beyond the image and into its meaning. Meanwhile, Ataullah introduced him to the writing of Austrian poet Rainer Maria Rilke, in particular *Letters to a Young Poet* (1929), which introduced a radical shift in how he perceived his own attempts at making art.

Burki learnt to hone his craft finely and graduated alongside the top students of his class, but he struggled to unite his interests and the knowledge that the very thing that brought him to art school ended up being pushed aside to make room for more elevated forms. Discontent with the state of theory instruction that couldn't help students contextualise the adoption of Western modernism movements by Pakistani artists post-independence, and the lack of modernisation of traditional forms, he left with more questions than answers about the fractures in our art history, and quite simply the disconnect between what we painted and why.

After Burki graduated from NCA in 2003, he continued painting in oils at his studio and experimented with various modes of expression. The visual language began to take on more graphic elements and some works seemed to directly reference a comic art sensibility, with and without cartoon figures. A subtler piece from 2004, *Untitled* [p. 34], stands out for me. Perhaps it is the men in uniform, or the large medal that forms the backdrop, and it surely has something to do with the cartoon explosion cloud, but the dull grey and green image looks like a study of a chalky Soviet war poster – an aesthetic not uncommon to graphic novels. Almost twenty years later, if you strip out the men, the cloud and other details, a sophisticated version of the composition and colour palette can be seen repeated in *Interval I*, 2017, [p. 35] part of Burki's more recent abstract series that are devoid of figures and symbolic forms.

In the mid-to-late 2000s, as he exhausted his fixation with oil paint and canvas, Burki moved towards working with paper. He initially drew upon his formal techniques and style, but soon realised that paper has its own agency, absorbing and warping in a way that canvas doesn't, and the larger its size the more difficult it became to control. But, Burki says, paper was a revelation. It not only challenged the way he worked with scale but also allowed him to shed a lot of unnecessary baggage and find room to express himself more freely. The medium was more responsive to spontaneity, and apart from it signalling a return to his illustrative roots, it also fed his preoccupation with the traditional format of miniature painting and book arts.

After they graduated, Burki and Mumtaz shared a studio space for almost five years, during which there was a much freer and more informed exchange of ideas. At the time, Mumtaz was a contributing arts writer for *The Friday Times*, and a vocal critic of contemporary miniature practices stemming from Pakistan.[3] All of this seeped into the ways in which Burki was painting, but he was particularly enamoured of Mumtaz's copy of the *Hamzanama* (also known as *Dastan-e-Amir Hamza*, published in 1855),[4] an epic narration of the adventures of Hamza (c. 569–625 CE), famed for its richly illustrated manuscript, which continues to influence miniature painters and Urdu novelists alike.

[3] *The Friday Times*, an English-language independent newsweekly based in Lahore, Pakistan.

4

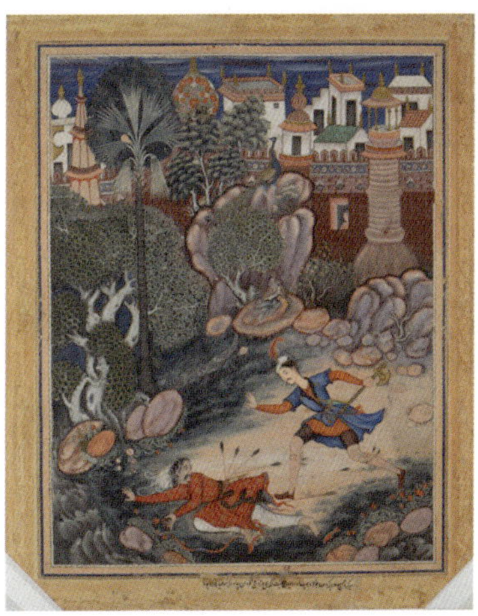

Umar Walks Around Fulad Castle, Meets a Foot Soldier and Kicks Him to the Ground. Folio from a *Hamzanama (The Adventures of Hamza)*, attributed to Kesav Das, c. 1570. Ink, opaque watercolour, and gold on cloth, mounted on paper, 73 × 56.5 cm. Collection of The Metropolitan Museum of Art, New York.

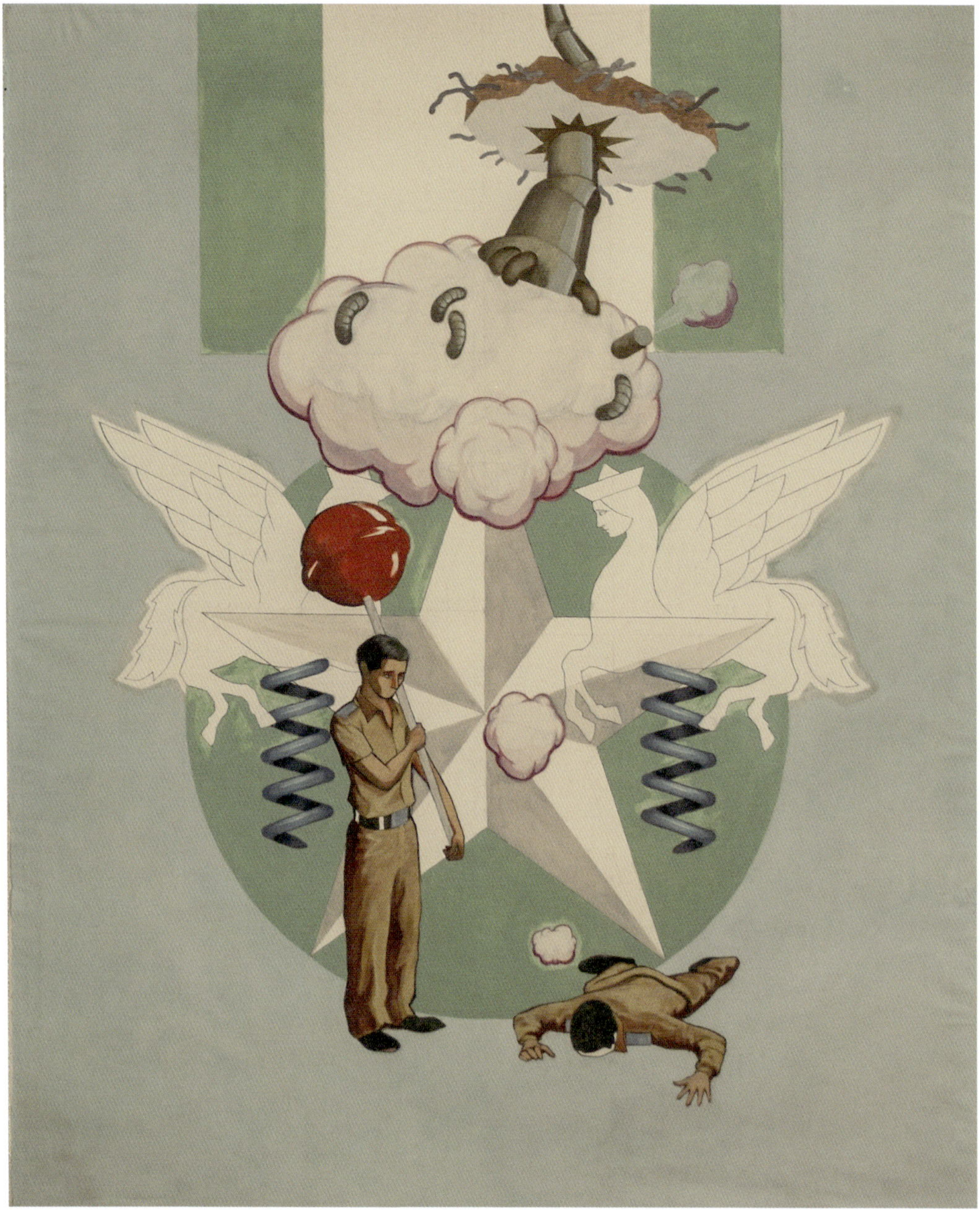

Untitled, 2004, oil on canvas, 165 × 137 cm

Interval I, 2017, acrylics, gesso and pencil on canvas, 56 × 44 cm

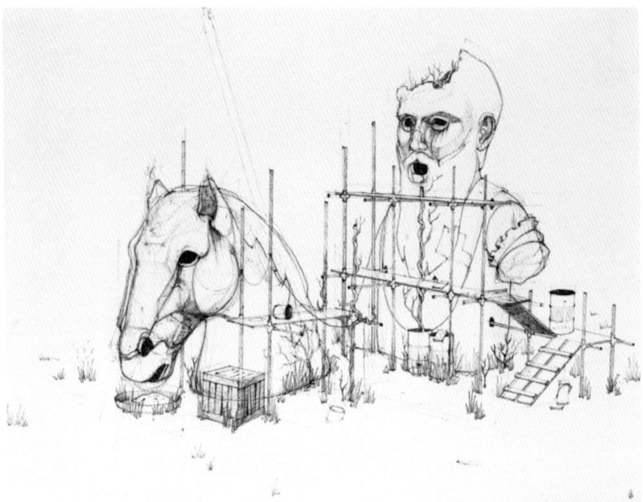

Drawing for Site, 2007, ballpoint pen on paper, 50.6 × 66.9 cm

Conversations around metaphysics and spirituality were fulfilling a personal schism but it was in *The Cult of Man* exhibition in 2007 [pp. 36-39] that Burki seemed to reconcile his interest in science fiction and his desire to explore the possibilities of miniature painting. The inspiration for the work itself stemmed from the poet and playwright Derek Walcott's version of *The Odyssey* (1993), which Burki cites as being deeply influential to his practice at the time.

In a completely transformed way of painting, he began employing a flat and empty background in which perspective and depth became arbitrary and, with extreme precision, rendered meticulously smooth, full-frontal forms on top that were part anthropomorphic, part phantasm. He chose to discard elements of the exotic and the orientalist, instead replacing them with ambiguous forms coloured in absurdity and humour. For the first time since he had started painting, the images were devoid of lifelike human figures. What persisted though was Burki's obsessive questing for perfection, an aspect I think he enjoys greatly and continues to manifest in his recent colour field and architectural paintings.

Soon after, when Burki joined the Royal Academy Schools in London, he was already working extensively with paper and had produced a large body of work independently. But it was at the RA Schools that, despite facing numerous challenges, Burki finally accepted paper as a medium in its entirety, embracing its nature as an imperative part of the work. It was a pivotal moment when Burki began to concentrate on the medium and let it take precedence over the image. Warping, he realised, was beautiful.

One of the major influences within Burki's visual language has been monumental architecture, which is also the mainstay of popular fantasy and sci-fi imagination – genres that Burki cites as source material. In real life, monumentalism is relegated to construction that occupies a public space in a large, impactful manner and seeks to memorialise something. It is not meant to be utilitarian and is often a site or sight that one visits to invoke memory and awe. In science fiction, this idea is turned on its head when the monumental isn't always relegated to the ceremonial. The repeated appearance of the monolith in *2001: A Space Odyssey*, for example, also serves a purpose. And so do the epic-scale constructions and designs for off-Earth colonies, interstellar travel, space wars and terraforming exercises in other films, books, and video games. As we got to talking about which narrative took this form to extremes, Burki and I both

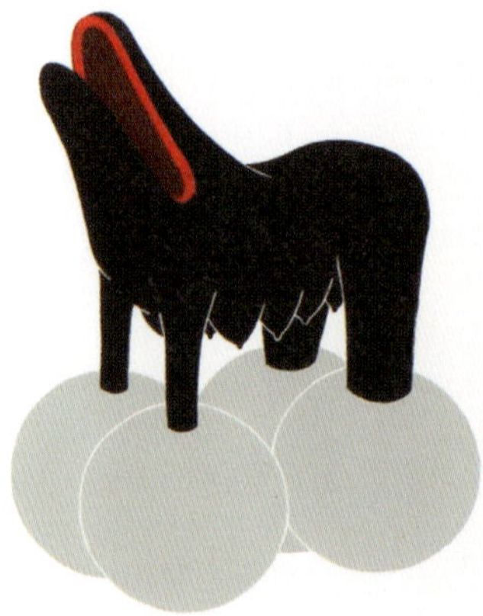

Untitled (dog), 2007, acrylics on paper, 40 × 30 cm

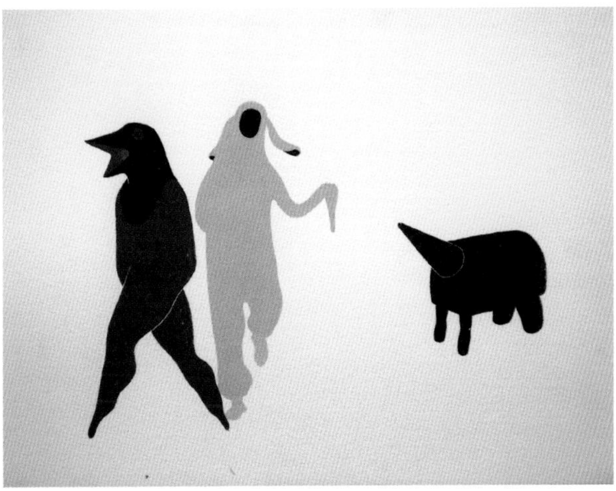

Troupe, 2007, acrylics on paper, 30 × 40 cm

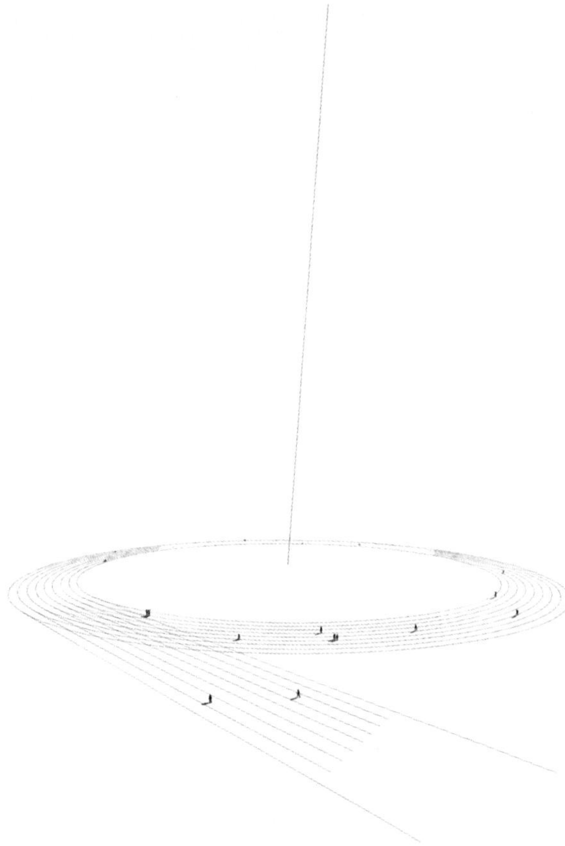

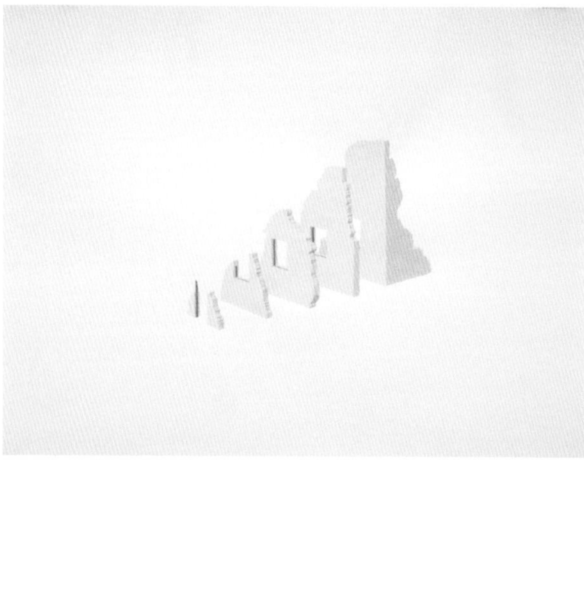

Parameter, 2008, felt tip pen and pencil on paper, 213 × 152 cm
Echo, 2008, acrylics on paper, 76 × 101 cm

were quick to refer to Clarke's 1973 novel *Rendezvous with Rama* – a story about a massive celestial object that measures 50 × 20 kilometres, weighs more than ten trillion tons, and enters the solar system for a fly-by – the first story that got me hooked on science fiction.

There is a paralysing power that is attached to monolithic shapes in our collective imagination. They have been at the heart of our religious beliefs, pinnacles from which kingdoms were ruled, signposts for claiming land, and totems of the unnamed dead. When they occur naturally, or exist from before memory, they become shrouded in mystery: impenetrable, dense, terrifying; symbolic of something great, gateways to more. Monumentalism here may seem unyielding, but it is functional. The scale is meant to inspire both reverence and dread, which can be recognised as tools for submission, especially in science fiction. For me, this is the world that Burki seems to reference when he creates his own monuments.

Although I refer to the rocky landscape from *2001: A Space Odyssey* as a visual device to enter Burki's works, such as *Tract I*, the film's more recognisable monolithic form is more discernible as a motif in the artist's oeuvre over the years. Much like their representation in literature and films, the monoliths in Burki's works also embody the burden of the viewer's perception. Is the unknown object non-human, and if so, does that make it divine?

In *Mother*, 2007, [p. 42] a thin white building reaches up to the skies, where a large, dark airship hovers, tethered to the apex. Most tall buildings can be seen as phallic symbols and typify man's attempt at staking dominance over the land and its people. When I speak to Burki about this work he uses words to the contrary. To him, the tall white column is like an umbilical cord, the large, attached zeppelin, a form that feeds from it. He calls it a mechanical deity and I immediately think of stories of dystopian futures where AI have subsumed many of society's necessary constructs, the 'nurturing' role becoming androgenised or deified, not necessarily female or maternal.

The zeppelin also lives on in steampunk and fantasy, but for many, it is a reminder of times past and ill-fated voyages like that of the *Hindenburg* tragedy of 1937. Burki admits that he finds the idea of the zeppelin, and its colossal shadow on the land below, extremely haunting. As a result, the ominous quality of *Mother* seems more suited to the bleakness of Philip K. Dick (here, I am reminded of his 1962 novel *The Man in the High Castle*) than to the techno-optimism of Clarke.

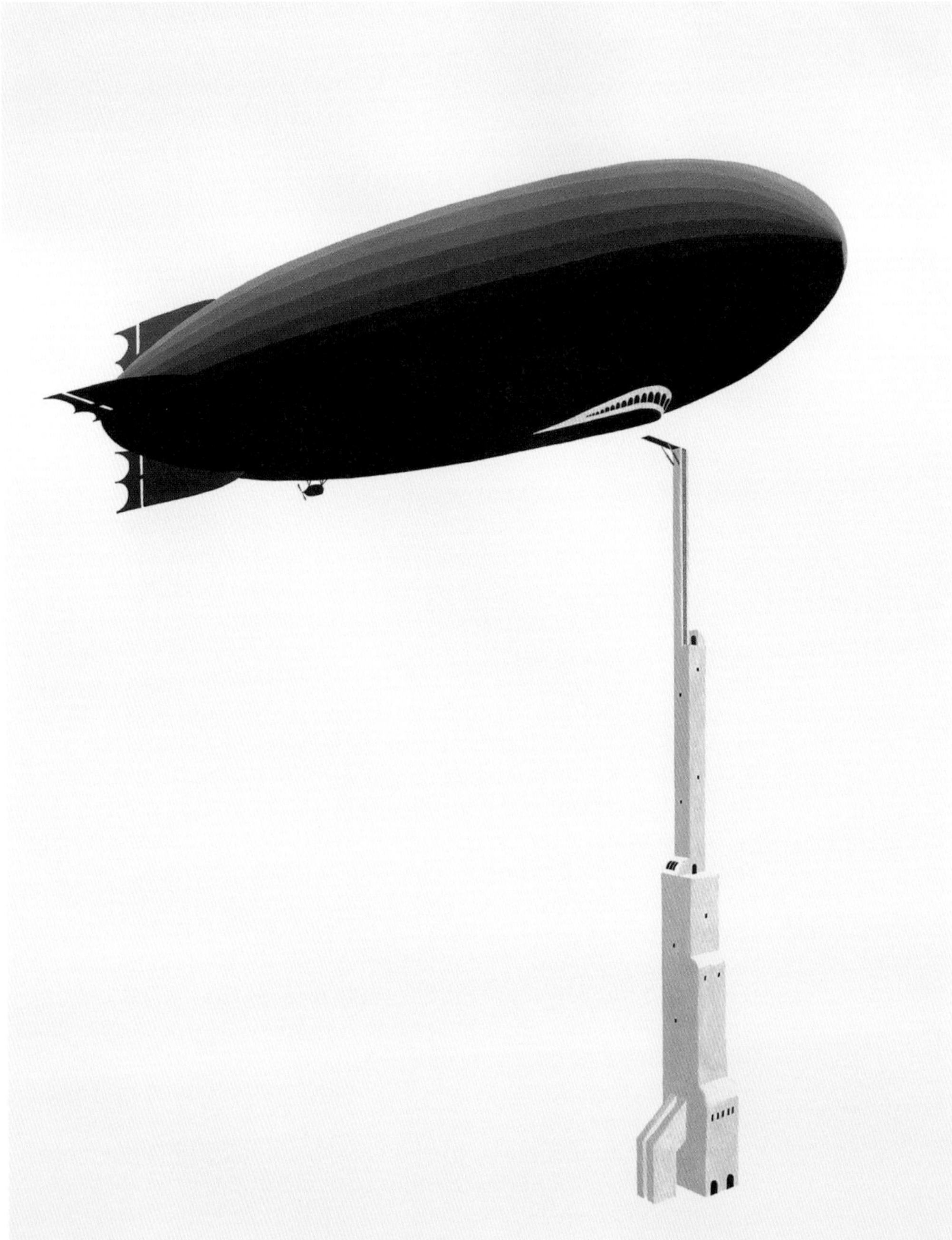

Mother, 2007, acrylics on paper, 76 × 50 cm

The symbolism in these structures continues with Burki's preoccupation with worship, rituals, meaning, disconnect, and fear of the unknown. Like millions of people in our country, we were born into the reverence of a monolith, to a backdrop of the call to prayer in a language that we do not speak nor understand. The impenetrability of many of these symbols makes way for them to be manifested in fiction, where we can learn to perceive rituals as a composite of abstract moments, movements and sounds.

Painted three years before the Burj Khalifa skyscraper was erected, *Mother* is oddly prophetic about illustrating the effect the tallest building in the world has on the people who live in its shadow. It is cruelly sharp, yet incredibly beautiful; it watches over the city like a new-age Christ the Redeemer, but is also a beacon to the lives it took; it is man-made, and still it is the Tower of Babel on days when its peak is lost in the clouds. Burki wasn't thinking of this building when he made *Mother*, but it feels like a blueprint that is surprisingly common to all such forms – heralding the glory and possibility of human superiority, that is foreshadowed by doom from its very beginning.

My entry into science fiction literature was by way of yellowing publications that I found in my great-uncle's house or at the old bookstore. As a teenager, I had no context of the post-war imaginary worlds of American and English authors, nor any critical understanding of what it meant for the white male protagonists to want to 'colonise' space in the quest for progress. Much of this I have learnt over time, and today the books read differently, but it does not make me want to discard them – primarily because without the iconic stories of Clarke, Dick, Frank Herbert and Isaac Asimov, science fiction discourse in mainstream culture would not exist. Thankfully, the world attempts to correct this unbalanced narrative – to one that is written by, and should belong to all – by bringing to me the important voices of women, African Futurism and Desi speculative fiction. And I delight in their frames of reference which resonate easily in the inherent social and cultural knowledge that exists *within* me.

Burki speaks of the *ritual* and although he mentions it in reference to ceremonial practices that have developed from cultural interpretations of religion, I believe that a lot of it can also be extended to our belief in, or knowledge of, the paranormal. We may lead seemingly pragmatic and earthly lives but, for example, it is not unusual to be blessed by family elders blowing Quranic verses

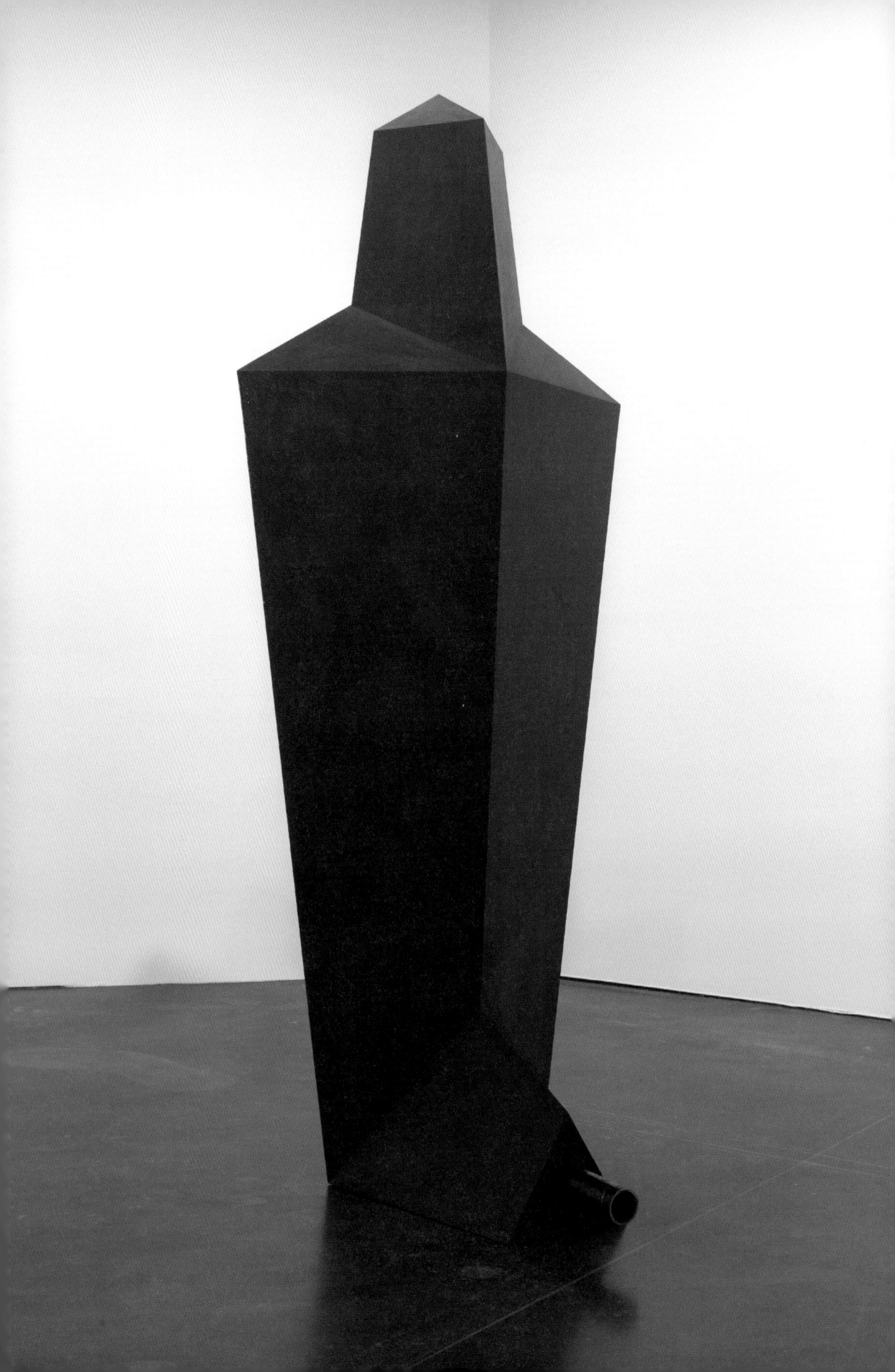

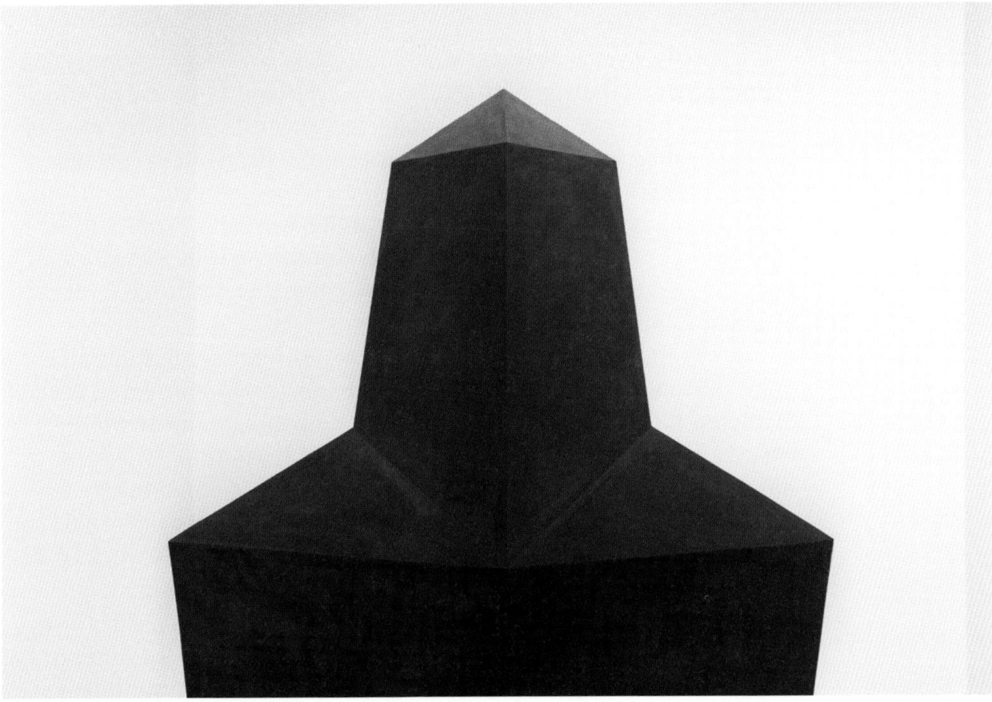

Each to Their Own, 2011, cedar, chipboard, MDF, charcoal and steel pipe, 249 × 112 × 97 cm

upon our foreheads or on drinking water to protect us from evil eye, black magic and non-human entities, like *jinn*. Or, instinctively practising learned behaviour like tying long hair at night, avoiding stepping under old trees after dark, being suspicious of exceptionally tall people who appear out of nowhere, and on it goes.

I discover that Burki has a long-lying interest in demonology, including a fascination with malevolent spirits in Japanese culture, and I can't help but conclude that he, too, pastures upon the *known* and normalised speculative realism present within our vernacular, and which include the dominions of *jinn, bhoot, churail, jadoo* and *chilla katna*, amongst others. Except, in his work, he marries these latent elements into forms with which he more readily identifies, ones that have come to us from the cold, hard, aspirational science of space-coloniser television.

Some of the more prevalent tropes represented in our popular imaginary and pulp fiction are: shadowy, elongated bodies; distorted figures that float weightlessly; eroticism of the possessed; spectrum of lights; long hair, longer nails; divination by way of numbers; and imaginary circular forms marking out safe spaces for solitary meditations. All of which I can find in my personal readings of Burki's images. Descriptive texts of Burki's work often avoid identifying such markers and details, which I think stems from his distaste for both the literal and the gimmicky. But from the minute I stood in front of the dark, spectral form of *Each to Their Own*, 2011, [pp. 44-45] I could feel a palpable ominousness that didn't need to be defined by a wall text. To date, it remains one of my favourite works by Burki, and also his most terrifying.

Holding up his green cyclops MS-06 Zaku II,[5] a robot from the Gundamverse, Burki animatedly tells me of his ambivalent relationship with the toy. He grew up frightened of this character but recounts how robots captured his interest from a young age and permeated his earliest illustrations. He now counts this particular mobile SUIT as one of his most prized possessions.[6] Not known to many outside his own circle, Burki has for years been slowly amassing a collection of Japanese toys and robots in his studio. It is not something he connects to his practice, but I disagree. Before he moved completely to non-representational imagery, robotic and anthropomorphic forms appeared quite often in his work, in some variation or another. This is the link.

5

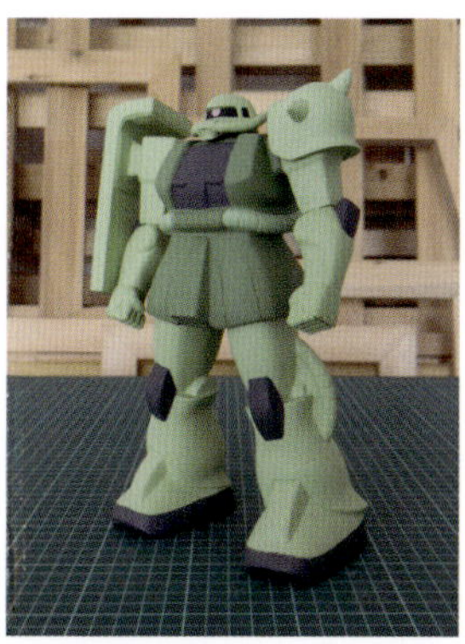

Bandai soft vinyl MS-06 Zaku II from the animated series *Mobile Suit Gundam*, 1979.

[6] SUIT, an acronym for Space Utility Instrumental Tactical.

One of the things that has happened over the years is that a certain vocabulary has developed around Burki's work that describes it in an almost sterile way. There are numerous references to a stark, graphic sensibility and flatness, or to deliberate arcaneness. A lot of it is down to Burki's own reluctance to speak about the works, or to narrativise the imagery and his process. In some ways, it is refreshing in an environment where the tendency is to over-explain content and context, and it does allow for a freer reading of the works. It is also satisfying to see people struggling to compartmentalise his work into contemporary Pakistani art, South Asian art, or Islamic art. But I believe the asceticism also locks the works down further, making them almost inscrutable. To decode Burki's brand of ambiguity, one must unravel the context within which it occurs. It is not necessary to posit an argument based on Eastern-versus-Western binaries, or how symbols can or cannot be identified directly within his work. What is more important, I believe, is to understand the world within which Burki creates, and the language that he may have developed in response to things he has adopted or struggled with.

Burki doesn't stick to a particular style or imagery for too long and his work is constantly changing. The only things that are consistent are the pleasure he takes in his 'non-art' interests and the questions he keeps asking himself: *why do I paint; what does the proliferation of the image mean; and, if an algorithm can produce abstract art, what value does intention hold?* In his quest, he has reduced painting to its most basic form, making the surface and structure an integral part of the image. I have no doubt that when he is done distilling, he will return to another form in which these borrowed monsters may reappear.

—

Deep in the human unconscious is a pervasive need for a logical universe that makes sense. But the real universe is always one step beyond logic." – Frank Herbert, *Dune* (1965)

Dawn, 2015, acrylics and pencil on paper, 76 × 56 cm

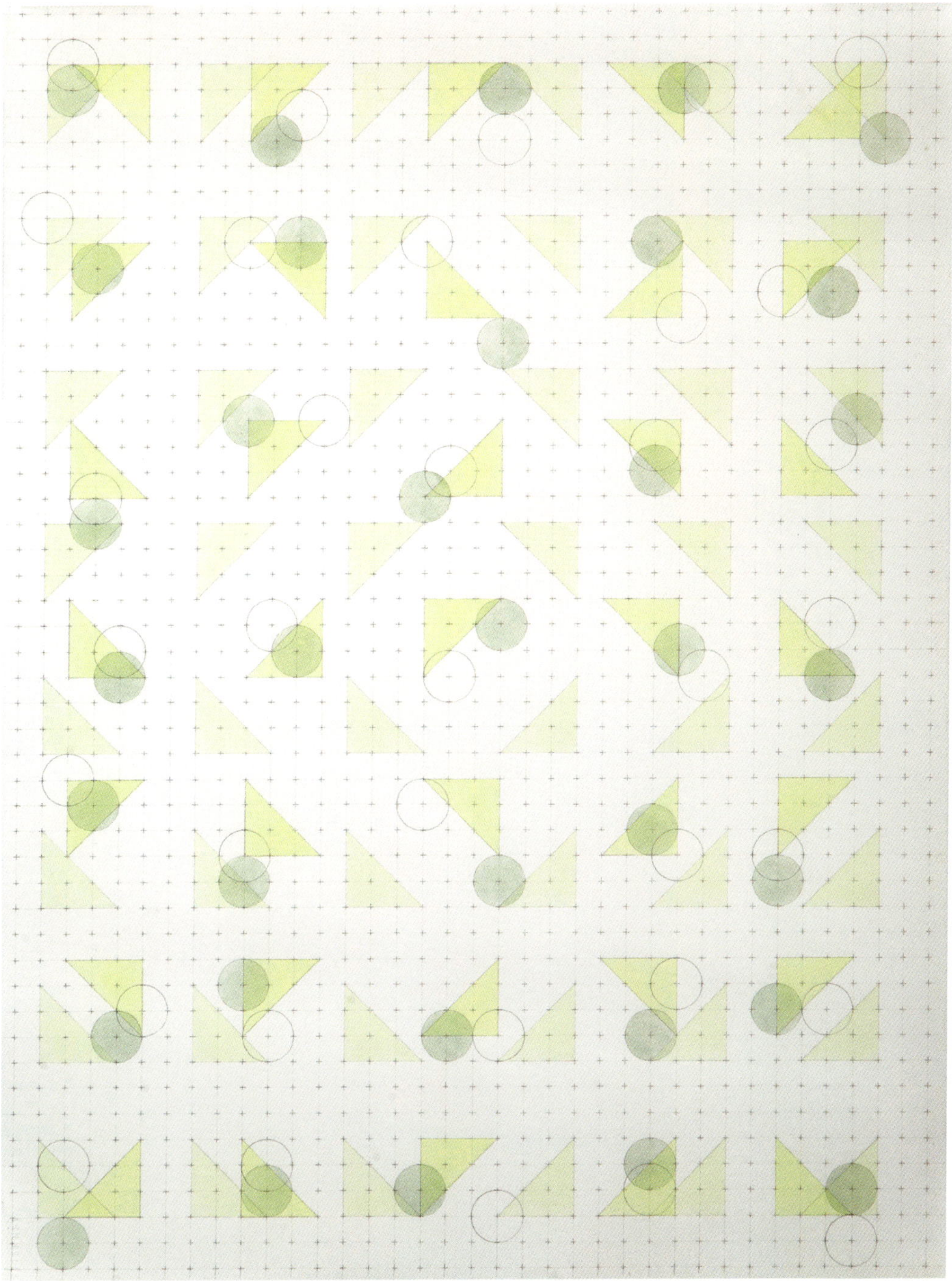

Noon, 2015, acrylics and pencil on paper, 76 × 56 cm

Beautiful Day, 2015, acrylics and pencil on paper, 76 × 56 cm

Journey, 2015, acrylics and pencil on paper, 76 × 56 cm

Ardor, 2015, acrylics and Indian ink on canvas, 183 × 183 cm

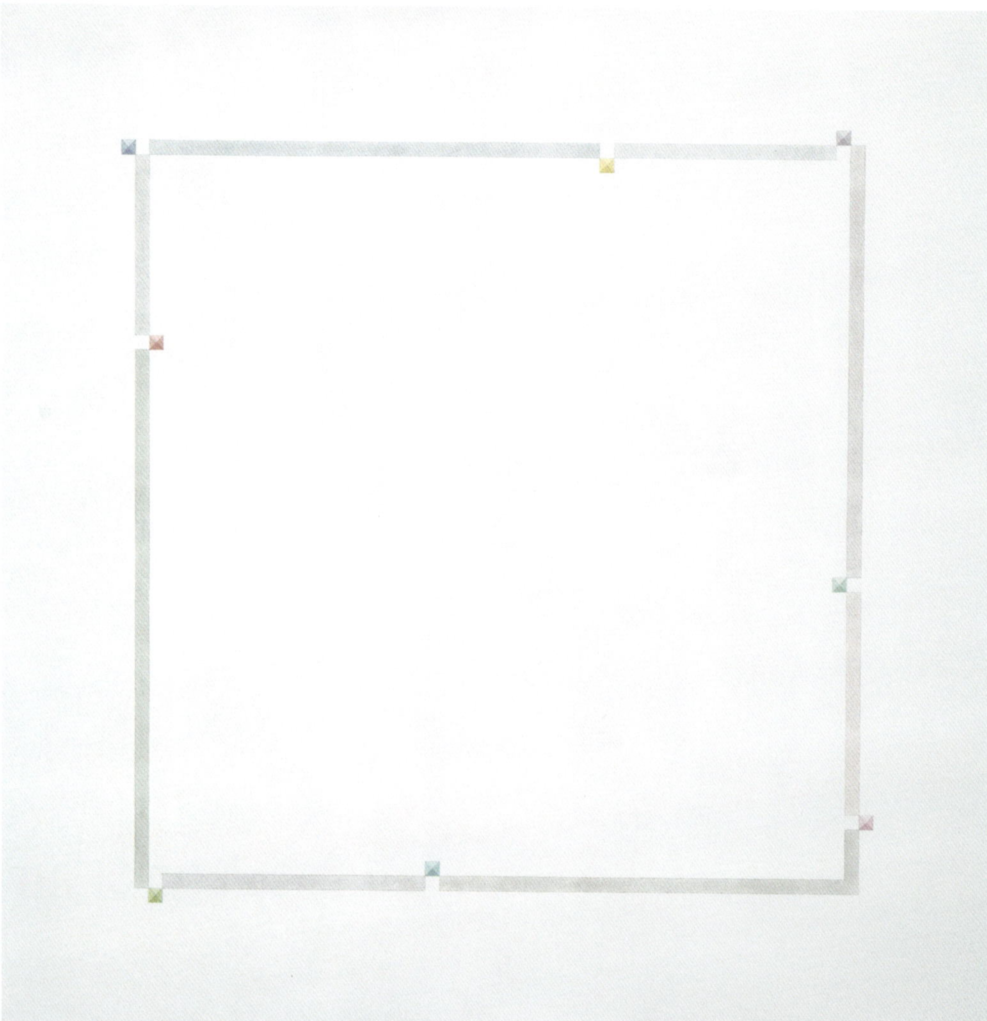

Elation, 2015, acrylics and pencil on canvas, 183 × 183 cm

Clearing, 2015, acrylics and pencil on paper, 76 × 56 cm

Untitled V, 2016, acrylics and pencil on paper, 122 × 152 cm

Fairweather, 2016, graphite pencil and acrylics on paper, 56.5 × 68.5 cm

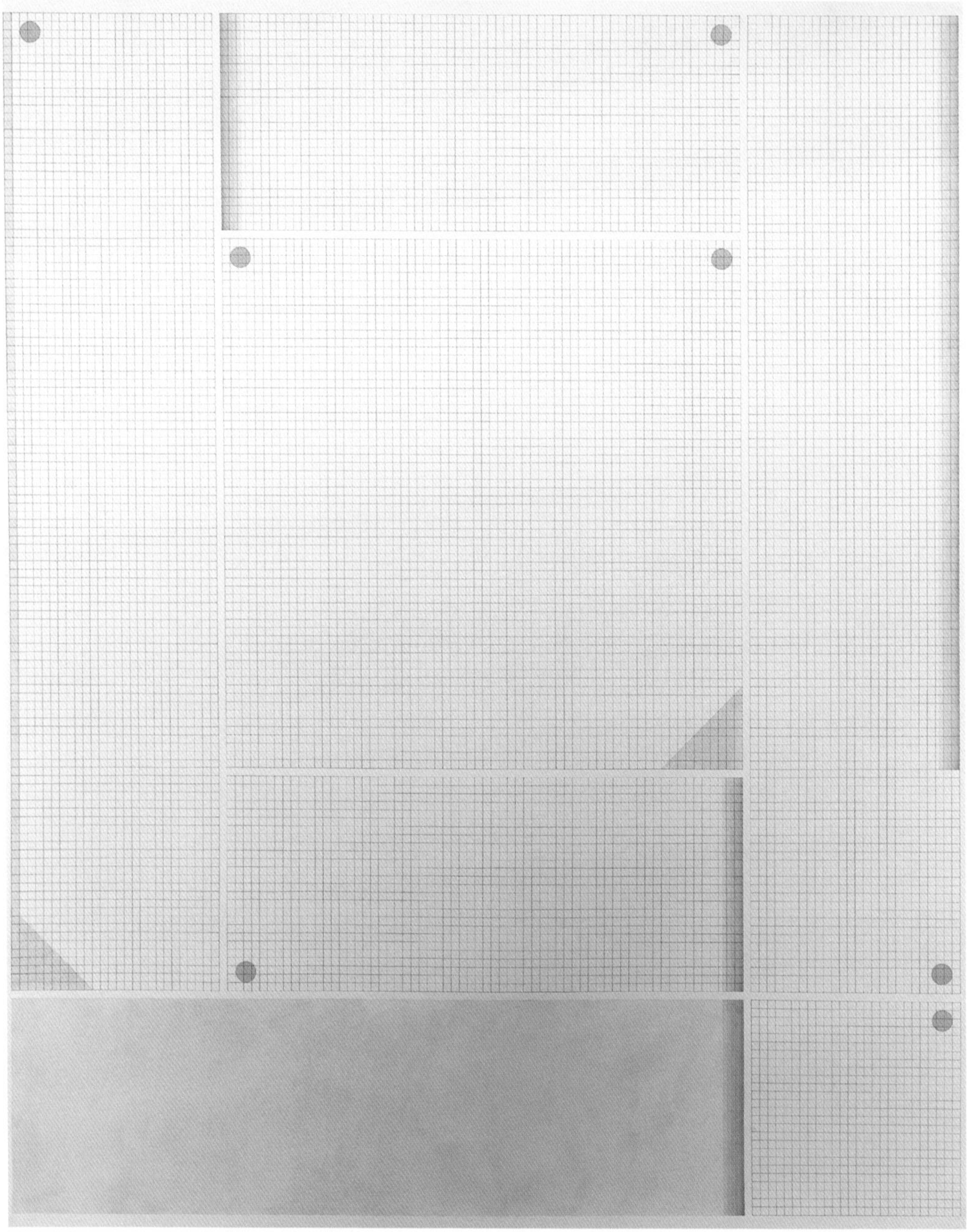

Park, 2016, acrylics and pencil on paper, 152 × 122 cm

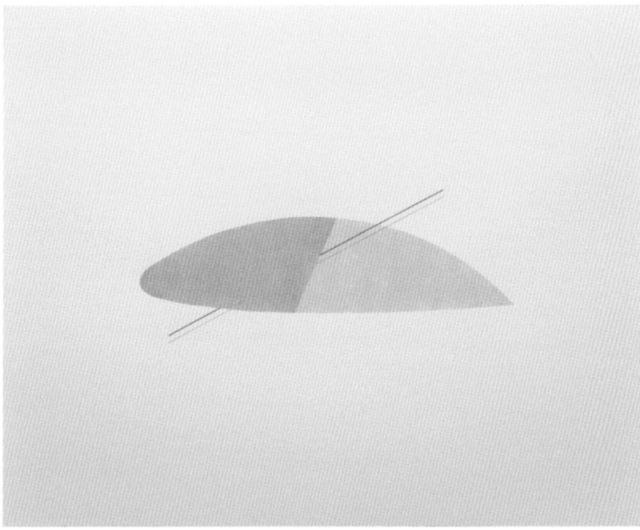

Momentary Structure V, 2017, acrylics and coloured pencil on paper, 38 × 48 cm

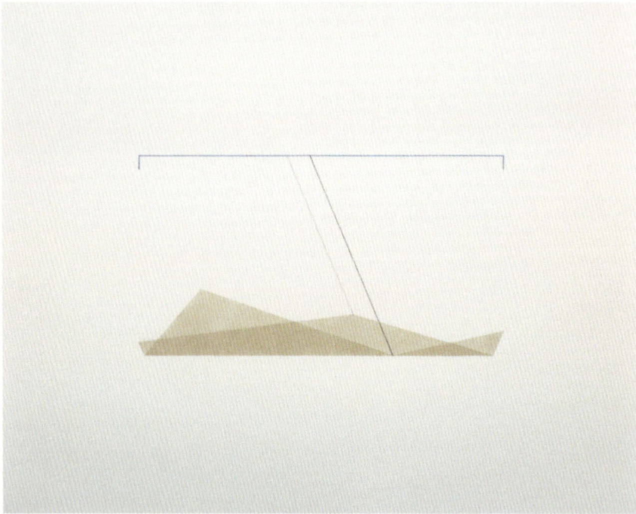

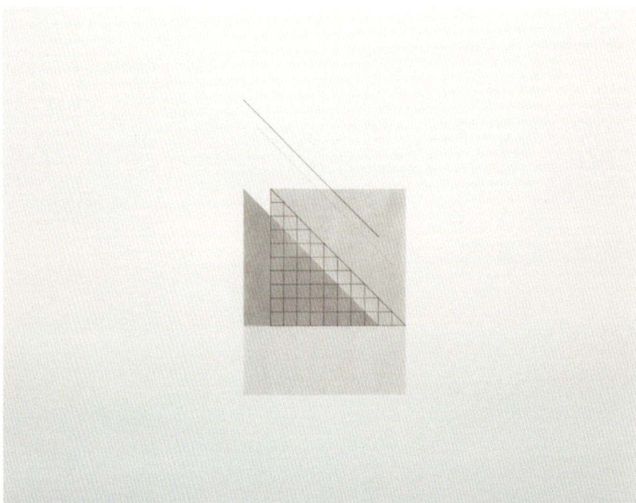

Momentary Structure VI, 2017, acrylics, pen and coloured pencil on paper, 38 × 48 cm
Momentary Structure VIII, 2017, acrylics, pen and coloured pencil on paper, 38 × 48 cm

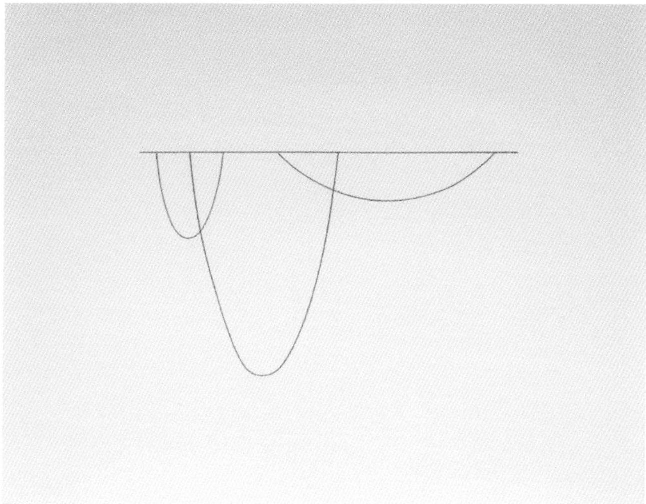

Momentary Structure X, 2017, coloured pencils on paper, 38 × 48 cm

Momentary Structure XI, 2017, acrylics and coloured pencil on paper, 38 × 48 cm

Untitled, 2017, graphite pencil and acrylics on paper, 57.5 × 76.5 cm

Interval II, 2017, acrylics, gesso and pencil on canvas, 59 × 44 cm

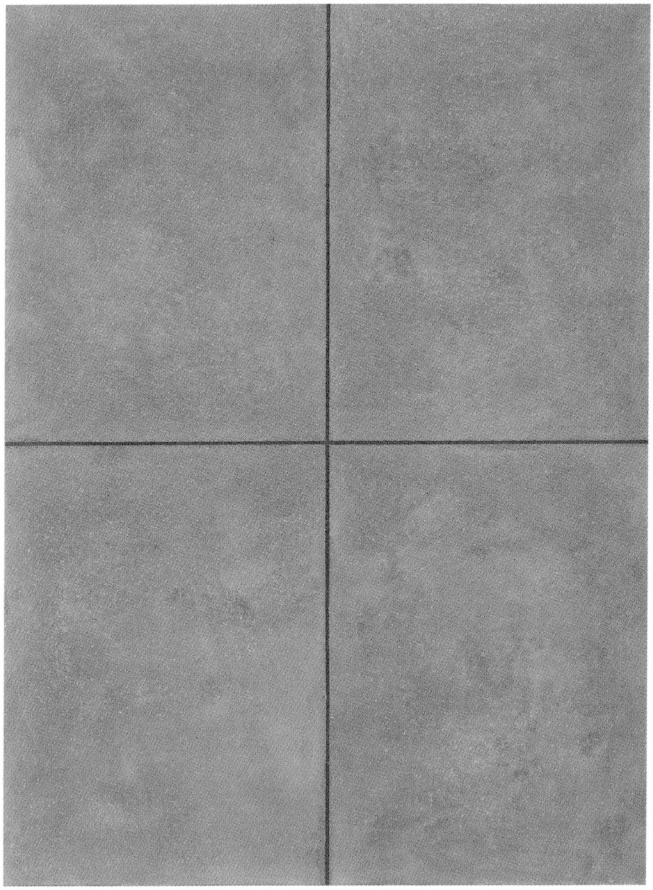

Interval V, 2017, acrylics, gesso and pencil on canvas, 59 × 44 cm

THE FADE
On Fahd Burki's Minimalism

Murtaza Vali

As an artistic position, minimalism can easily become dogmatic, the rigour and precision it requires stifling innovation and breeding a type of aesthetic stasis. In contrast, Fahd Burki's almost decade-long foray into minimalist abstraction, reveals itself in retrospect to be marked by near constant experimentation. Though committed to an economy of line, form and colour, his abstract work is filled with reversals, contradictions and paradoxes. Though experimental, it is rarely processual. Each composition is carefully planned, often refined and finalised digitally before being executed precisely by the artist's own hand or carefully fabricated by collaborators according to his specifications. Very little is ever left up to accident or chance, and signs of process are never visible in the final object. Yet, there are significant conceptual, formal, and material shifts between bodies of work. And while Burki's abstractions are intentionally quiet and minimal they also always teeter on the edge between non-objectivity and representation. Suggesting subtle ways in which the reductive language of geometric abstraction can be opened up to spatial and temporal complexities, these works hold on to the possibilities of narrative and metaphor, an abiding interest that Burki acknowledges.[1] In this essay, I examine one such strategy, which recurs as trope, technique and methodology across his experiments in minimalist abstraction, what I call the 'fade'.

The fade is a tonal or chromatic gradation, a gradient effect, and instances of it can be found in both Burki's non-objective and representational work, and across the many mediums he has employed. Indebted to manga and anime, his figurative and iconic works display a strong graphic sensibility and are largely composed of flat, solid blocks of paint. However, if you look carefully enough, you will notice the fade appear and disappear, again and again.[2] Sometimes it is broken down into discrete increments, suggesting a stepwise progression, as on the upper part of the zeppelin in *Mother*, 2007, [p. 42] where it suggests the airship's volume, its horizontal ribs creating a kind of stylised shading effect. In *Untitled*, 2012, [p. 72] the face or snout of the rabbit-like creature appears as a sectioned upside-down triangle that, while shifting from a light to darker grey, also remains resolutely flat. Other times it appears as a smooth continuous gradient, as in the coral to light-blue beak-like form in *Healer*, 2012, [p. 73] or the hollow eye sockets in the light-blue skull

[1] Fahd Burki, personal communication, 18 January 2022.
[2] For more detailed discussion of Burki's early figurative work, see Murtaza Vali, 'Fahd Burki: Prostheses/ thejamjar in association with GREYNOISE', *ArtAsiaPacific* 70 (Sept.-Oct. 2010), 155; Murtaza Vali, 'Uncertain Icons', *Fahd Burki: Works From 2003–2013* (Dubai: Grey Noise; Milan: Skira, 2014), 174–181; and Saira Ansari, 'Borrowed Monsters', in this volume.

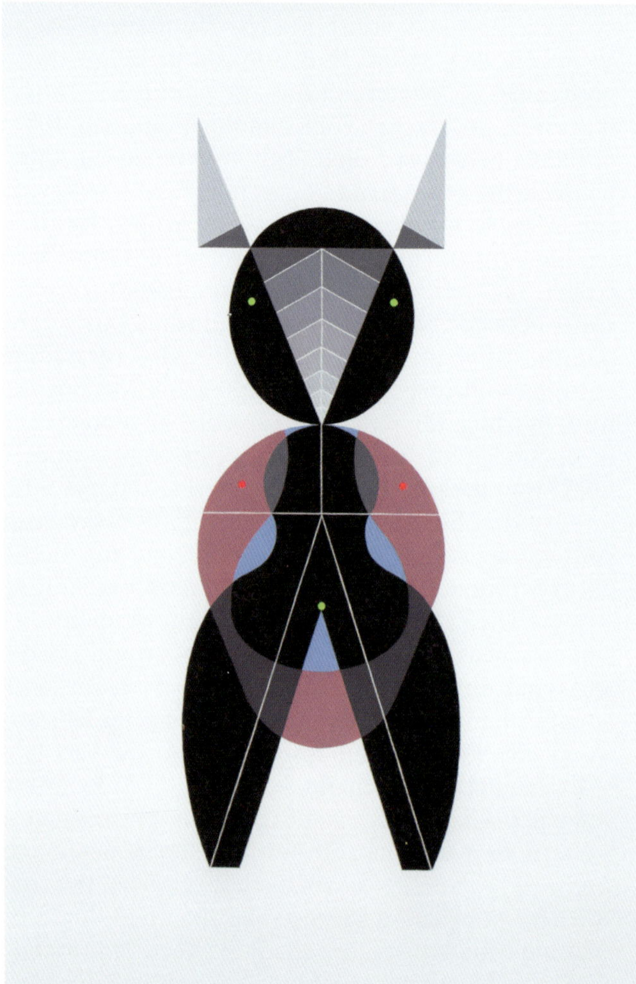

Untitled, 2012, acrylics on paper, 56 × 38 cm

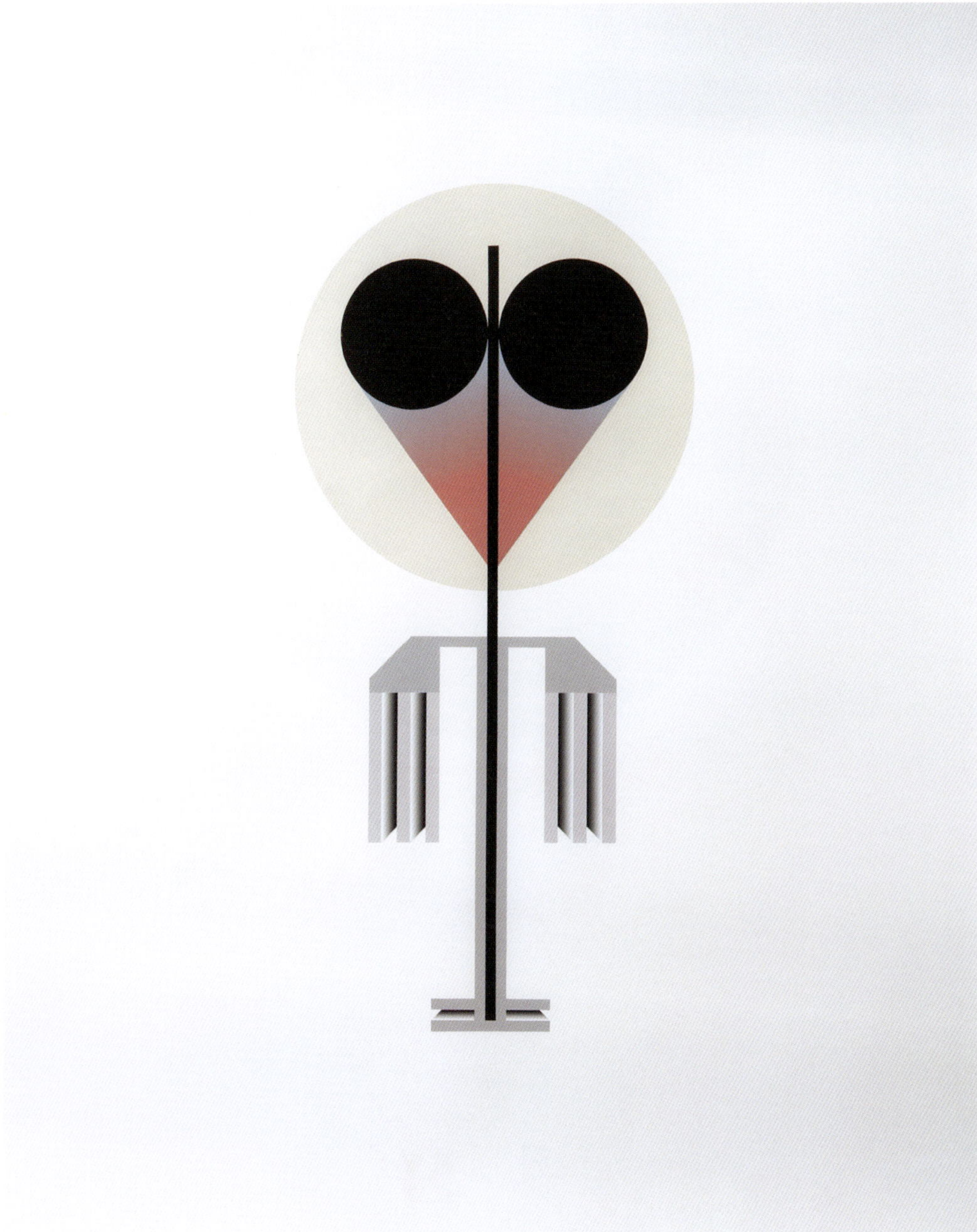

Healer, 2012, acrylics and collage on paper, 155 × 122 cm

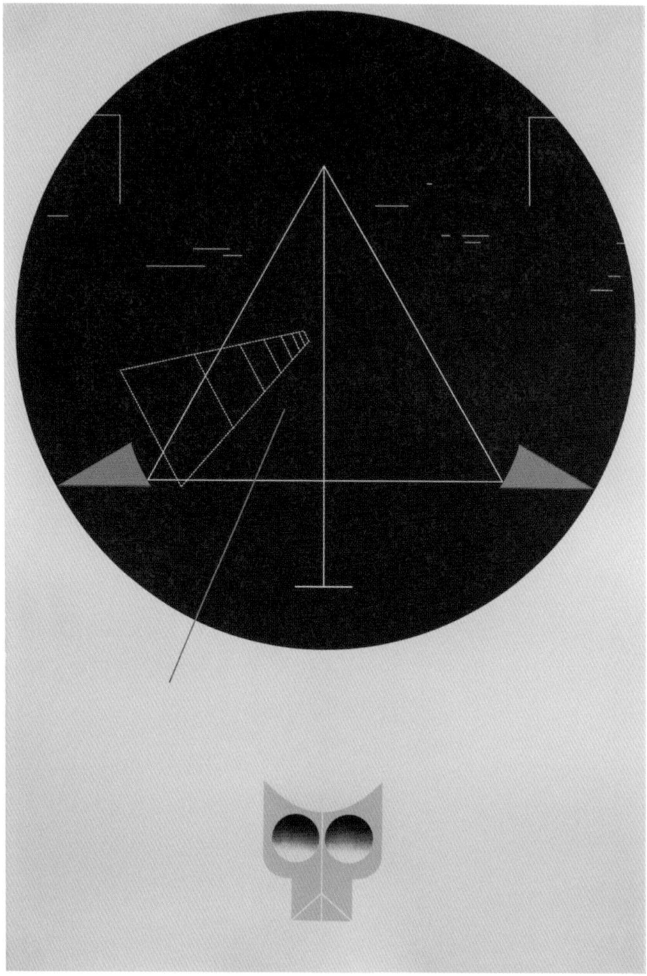

Night Walk, 2013, screen print on paper, 112.5 × 76.5 cm

at the bottom of *Night Walk*, 2013, [p. 74]. In *Toward Light*, 2013, [p. 77] a yellow circle and green cypress tree-shaped form dissolve into each other, the sublime experience of the light of the rising sun breaking through a thicket pared down into a logo. And in *Seeking Eden*, 2014, [p. 25] the sublime sky at sunset (or moonrise) is rendered through hundreds of ruled lines that shift in colour from white through light blue, pink, and lilac before darkening through purple to an almost midnight blue.

Roland Barthes's penultimate course at the Collège de France provides a useful frame through which to understand the mechanics and semantics of gradation. In those lectures, delivered between 1977 and 1978, Barthes develops a theory of what he calls the 'Neutral', challenging the oppositional binarism of structuralist and post-structuralist thought by shifting the frame of analysis to the interval in between, what he suggestively calls the 'stretching'.[3] For Barthes, the 'Neutral' delineates a terrain that is attentive to nuance, where shifts in quality and intensity, however small, gain in significance. The metaphor of extension implied in 'stretching' is useful in understanding Burki's recurrent use of gradation as a strategy. If we understand it spatially, it can suggest the illusion of depth and volume but also imply movement. But it can also be understood temporally. A visual gradient introduces the experience of time into abstract form. Characterised by flat planes, strong geometries, and vivid colours, much geometric abstraction, exemplified by the work of artists such as Carmen Herrera and Ellsworth Kelly, is declarative, imposing itself on our vision instantaneously. This is not to say that extended looking cannot enrich an encounter with such work but that the work itself does not appear to engender such commitment. In contrast, gradation slows down perception and cognition, as sight and mind must register, process, and adjust to each incremental shift. And, arguably, the spatial expansion and temporal dilation of the 'stretch' always hold the potential (or threat, depending on how dogmatic a definition of abstraction you subscribe to) for metaphor and narrative.

[3] Roland Barthes, *The Neutral: Lecture Course at the Collège de France* (1977–1978), trans. Rosalind E. Krauss and Denis Hollier (New York: Columbia University Press, 2005). I have also used Barthes' 'Neutral' as a theoretical frame through which to read Seher Shah's most recent 'grey' works. See Murtaza Vali, 'In the Grey', *Seher Shah: Of Absence and Weight* (New York: Rizzoli, 2022).

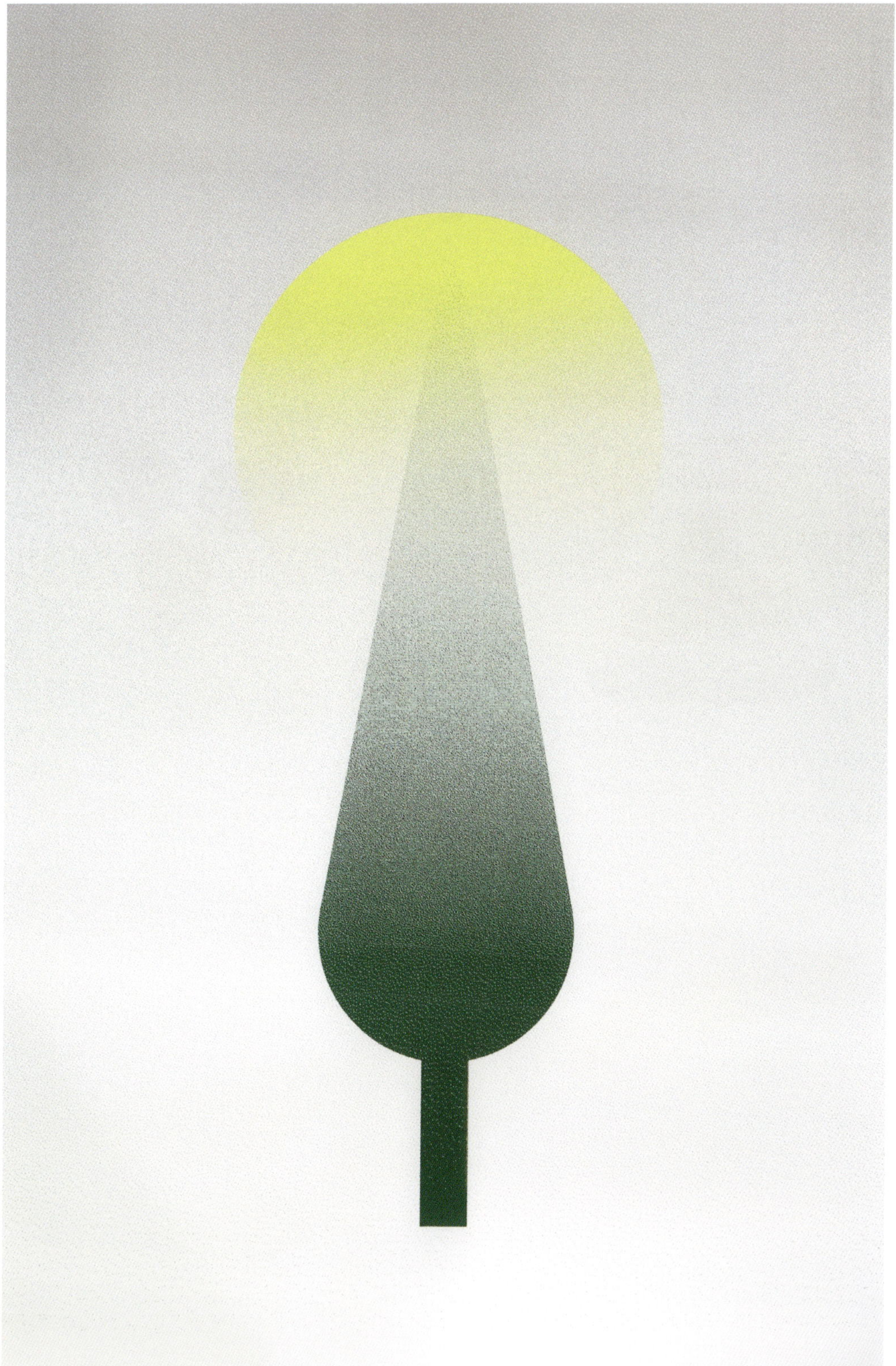

Toward Light, 2013, screen print on paper, 112.5 × 76.5 cm

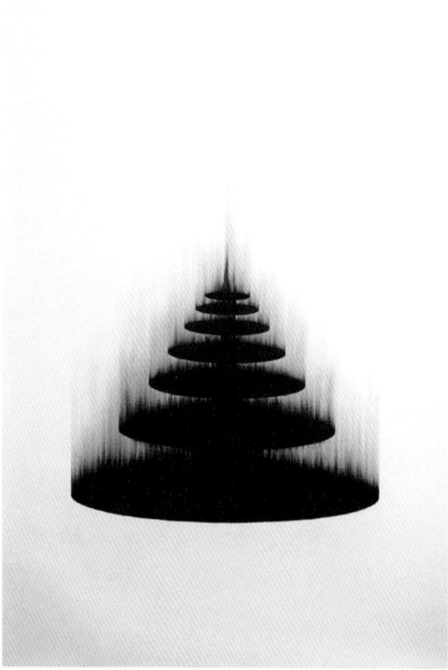

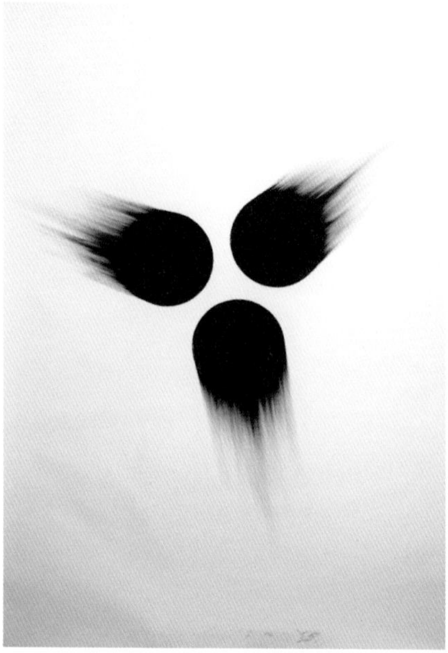

Combustion I, 2009, charcoal on paper, 213 × 152 cm
Combustion II, 2009, charcoal on paper, 213 × 152 cm

Blur, Glow, Whisper

Burki uses the capacity for the fade to imply movement in what are, arguably, his earliest abstractions, a pair of large charcoal-on-paper drawings titled *Combustion I* and *II*, 2009, [p. 78]. Part of a body of work related to death and cremation, Burki's use of charcoal – rare in his practice – was inspired by its material similarity to ashes.[4] *Combustion I* features a stack of seven dense black ovals that decrease in width from bottom to top, their shape and diminishing size suggesting a line of equally-sized circles receding into space. In *Combustion II*, three discs hover around an empty centre. In both drawings, Burki, taking advantage of charcoal's soft smudginess, carefully and selectively smears certain edges of the shapes: the top of each ellipse in the former, the outer curve of each circle in the latter. Blurring the rigid contours of gestalt geometries, this gesture adds the impression of movement to otherwise static forms. The ellipses appear to evaporate or smoulder; the three discs hurtle towards the centre. And with this suggestion of movement comes the possibility of narrative and metaphor. The fade transforms the circles into subatomic particles or celestial bodies moments before an inevitable collision. Diffusing upwards, the ellipses can be read metaphysically, suggesting transcendence or ascension.

For Barthes, the 'Neutral' privileges the precognitive and qualitative, and as such, is determined by and engenders both sense and affect.[5] To use his wonderfully evocative language, the 'Neutral' twinkles or shimmers. In the history of painting, gradation, beyond volume and movement, has often been used to picture light in landscape, especially the sublime and paradisiacal light of liminal moments such as dawn and dusk, a tradition Burki seems to evoke in works like *Toward Light* and *Seeking Eden*. But Burki has also used this shimmer in more abstract compositions, creating the illusion of lambent light through careful incremental shifts in tone and colour. Take *Saint*, 2011, [p. 80] another important transitional work between his figurative and abstract periods. A symmetrical iconic form composed of flatly painted sections in four marginally different light greys, it seems to glow, possibly inspiring its beatific title. Burki recreates the effect in *Radiance*, 2015, [p. 81] using a grid to systematise it while simultaneously disrupting its structural regularity by removing a tiny triangle from one of the corners of each square. The variable location of this cut results in

[4] For a longer discussion of these works, see Vali, 2014, 181. Note 2.

[5] For a discussion of the relationship between Barthes' 'Neutral' and affect theory, see Gregory J. Seigworth and Melissa Gregg, 'An Inventory of Shimmers', *The Affect Theory Reader*, eds. Melissa Gregg and Gregory J. Seigworth (Durham: Duke University Press, 2010), 10–12.

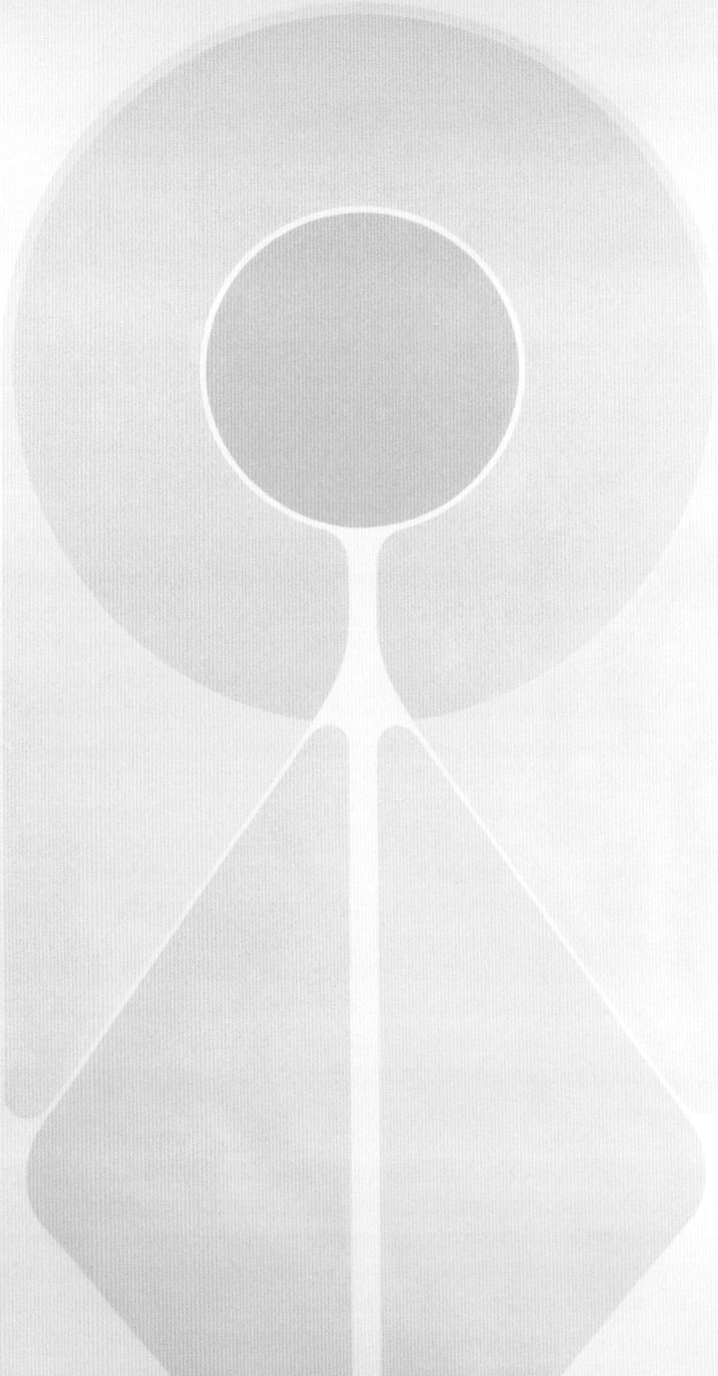

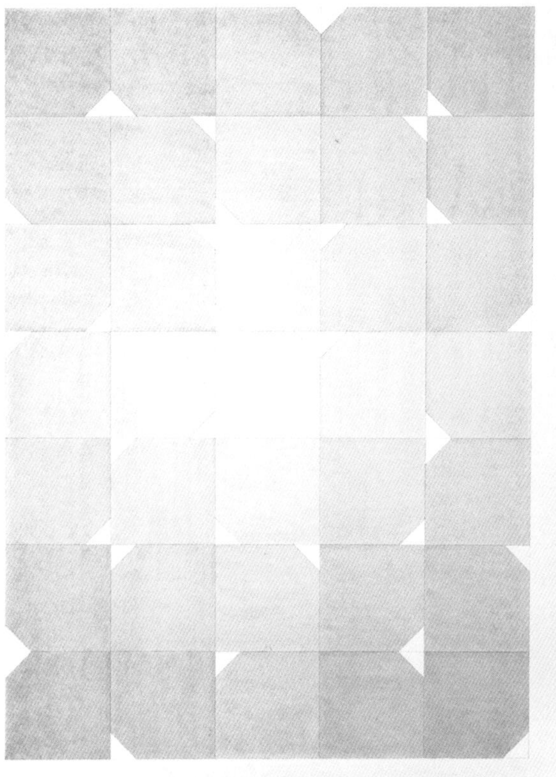

Radiance, 2015, acrylics and pencil on paper, 76 × 56 cm
(opposite) *Saint*, 2011, acrylics on paper, 218.44 × 139.7 cm

an unpredictable pattern and introduces a sense of play. Save the unmarked white one at the centre, each unit is a slightly different shade of greyish off-white, getting incrementally darker from the centre out. The visual effect, as the title acknowledges, is one of luminosity, a somewhat dappled glow.

If colour shouts in Herrera's and Kelly's paintings, Burki dials chroma down to a whisper in his. In his first presentation of wholly abstract works, in 2016, colour was muted and diffused, with thinned down acrylic washes used to paint delicately translucent lines and shapes, which sometimes overlapped and intersected to create further tonal complexity.[6] Like the fade, these hushed hues introduce an experience of time into otherwise fixed abstract forms and compositions. Colour is not simply present, but appears as an echo from the past, softened by the passage of time and exposure to the elements. It is the memory of colour or, rather, colour as memory itself. This wistfulness is made explicit in the titles, which evoke fleeting moments, experiences, or sensations: *Dawn*, *Noon*, *Beautiful Day*, *Journey*, *Ardor*, *Elation*, all 2015, [pp. 50-58]. Burki's subdued palette is reminiscent of Agnes Martin, especially the acrylic-on-canvas works she made after her return to painting in the early 1970s following a six-year hiatus.[7] Burki acknowledges this influence in works like *Rest*, 2015, [p. 84] and *Wander*, 2015, [p. 85] whose six-foot-square dimensions recreate Martin's preferred format since the early 1960s.

However, while Martin stayed committed to the grid as an organising element, Burki's use of it is less definitive, less dogmatic. It is sometimes implied but not drawn in, as in *Dawn* and *Noon*. Other times it appears incomplete or only occupies a portion of the composition, more symbol than structure. For example, while the top two thirds of *Rest* lacks verticals, a band at the bottom lacks horizontals and is topped with short alternating diagonals that create a row of triangles that prop up the grid above it. *Wander* almost entirely lacks verticals, save two thin red strips that run the entire height of the canvas, evoking the look of a ruled page in a notebook. And what initially appears as a field of parallel horizontals, reveals itself on closer looking as a zigzag, subtly expanding and contracting the space between the lines. In both of these works, Burki includes a prominent horizontal element two thirds of the way up the composition that, though abstracted, functions as a horizon. Two thin arctic-blue isosceles triangles, mirrored, are inset within a white band, floating like icebergs. A narrow frieze of overlapping triangles in gradations of pale green suggest a misty mountain range. In other works, a red or yellow circle suggests the sun. Burki seems to make Martin's ambiguous relationship to landscape and nature – one that she simultaneously evoked and denied throughout her career – explicit.[8]

From Line to Groove, From Centre to Periphery

In the following year, 2017, Burki abandoned the square format, the arrays of floating shapes, the parallel and intersecting lines. Rectangular and smaller in scale, the paintings are more focused, often pared down to just a few lines, as if he had simply zoomed in on a detail in one of the works that had preceded them. Accordingly, the lines gained the slightest illusion of depth, becoming shallow grooves, as if cut or etched into the surface, like the bevelled edge of a matte frame. Canvas becomes cardboard or stone, painting becomes bas-relief. And the translucent acrylic washes used to carefully fill in lines and shapes spill out of their contours and flood the picture plane. Paint is not applied as a discrete layer atop a surface, be it paper or canvas, but stains the support itself. *Interval II*, 2017, [p. 68] is blue-grey field bisected by a trio of horizontal beige stripes. In *Interval V*, 2017, [p. 69] the canvas is quartered, its muddy grey resembling stone or poured concrete. *Untitled*, 2017, [p. 86] is divided horizontally into thirds. Three short lines – two diagonals and a vertical – bisect each of the sections, activating the composition. Each band is a different colour – the top a pale slate-blue, the middle a hazy green, and the bottom a dewy golden yellow, with the warmth of dimming summer sunlight. Rather than a material fact, in these works colour appears as a ghost of itself, haunting the surface, floating in like a delicate mist or a light fog. Saturating but not entirely overwhelming the visual field, colour inhabits it, like atmosphere.

The year 2018 marked another significant shift, a return to the flatter, more opaque application of paint that characterised Burki's figurative works. In these paintings, Burki often leaves sections of the canvas unpainted but applies a clear matte gesso

[6] These first abstractions were exhibited under the title 'New Work' at Grey Noise, Dubai, March 14 – May 7, 2016. For a review of the show, see Murtaza Vali, 'Fahd Burki/Grey Noise', *Artforum* 55, no. 1, Sept. 2016, 384.
[7] Agnes Martin's use of colour was the focus of an exhibition at Pace Gallery, New York, May 5 – June 26, 2021. See Agnes Martin et al., *Agnes Martin: The Distillation of Color* (New York: Pace Publishing, 2022), especially Durga Chew-Bose, 'In Imagination Only', 41–54.
[8] For a critique of the way Agnes Martin's abstractions are read as analogues of nature or examples of the 'abstract sublime', see Rosalind Krauss, 'Agnes Martin: The /Cloud/', *Bachelors* (Cambridge, Mass.: MIT Press, 1999), 75–89.

Rest, 2015, acrylics and pencil on canvas, 183 × 183 cm

Wander, 2015, acrylics and pencil on canvas, 183 × 183 cm

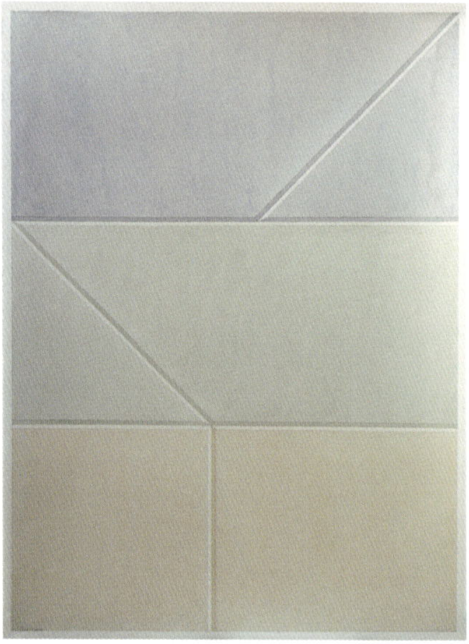

Untitled, 2017, graphite pencil and acrylics on paper, 76.5 × 57.5 cm
Gratitude, 2018, acrylic gesso on canvas, 100 × 76 cm

to them, so that the canvas appears to have a unified surface overall. The gesso stabilises the raw canvas while also minimising its woven texture, so it functions primarily as another colour.[9] Compositionally, these masterful paintings interrogate conventional distinctions between figure and ground, centre and periphery, through just a few rectilinear shapes. In *Gratitude*, 2018, [p. 86] a matte white rectangle fills much but not all of the canvas, leaving a narrow border of unpainted canvas around it.[10] This frame is interrupted by additional shapes. Thin white horizontal bands float just above and below the monolith, separated from it by strips of unpainted canvas of roughly the same thickness. A pair of equally-sized rectangles of pale blue, a smaller rectangle of unpainted canvas between them, flank the central shape on both sides. Though Burki carefully paints each different section of the canvas as flatly and evenly as possible, our eyes and mind instinctually connect aligned shapes of the same colour. The result is an illusion of overlap and the suggestion of depth, however shallow it might be, that accompanies it. The painting toggles between seemingly opposing qualities, between flatness and depth, abstraction and illusion, matter and metaphor. It is precisely this capacity to blur categories, to 'baffle the paradigm', that Barthes ascribes to the 'Neutral', and to the gradient as a manifestation of it.[11]

Untitled I, 2018, and *Untitled II*, 2018, [pp. 88-89] which share a compositional logic, trouble figure-ground relationships through placement not depth. In both, Burki repeats but inverts the same detail on opposite sides or corners of the canvas. In the former it is a vertical blue line whose thickness triples halfway along its height. The latter features a small flag-like rectangle, subdivided into a white square and a thin sky-blue stripe. Through these elements, Burki displaces the figure from its conventional locus at the centre of a composition to the periphery of the canvas. Our eyes, accustomed to anchoring themselves to a figure, are forced out to the edges. Though modest in scale, these paintings are strangely unsettling, the displacement of figure to the periphery intensifying our perception of the monochromatic field at the centre. The figure becomes frame. The centre becomes ground, absence, the void. These works mark the beginning of a sustained interrogation of the semantics of the frame. In *The Truth in Painting*, Jacques Derrida theorises the frame as *parergon*, a 'supplement' that both delineates and destabilises the

[9] Burki, personal communication.
[10] *Gratitude*. Interestingly, this painting shares its title with a late canvas by Agnes Martin from 2001.
[11] Barthes, 196. Note 5.

Untitled I, 2018, acrylic gesso on canvas, 84 × 64 cm

Untitled II, 2018, acrylic gesso on canvas, 84 × 64 cm

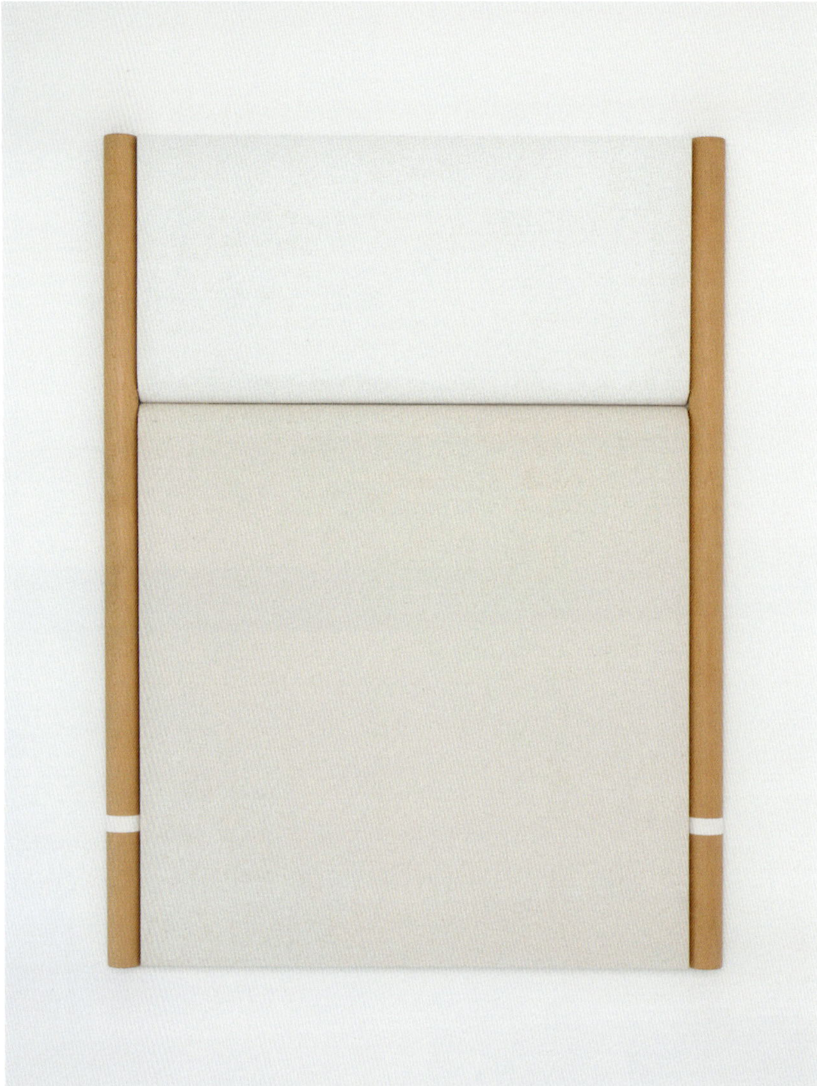

Minutes before I fall asleep, 2019, wood, canvas, acrylic paint, 100.2 × 77 × 4.2 cm

definition and limit of the work of art.[12] Burki illustrates Derrida's deconstructive approach brilliantly, experimenting with different strategies to blur the conceptual and literal distinction between frame and picture, inverting the traditional hierarchy between them, first visually and then physically.

Cut and Fade

Burki's next phase begins to reconcile the two seemingly opposing positions that preceded it: the illusion of three-dimensionality through a deepening of line into groove in the paintings from 2017 and the resolute flatness and blurring of figure-ground and centre-periphery hierarchies of the canvases that followed a year later. In a suite of hybrid works that hover between painting and sculpture, image and object, he makes these previously painterly investigations physical and material. The illusionistic grooves deepen further into real cuts, into both the surface and the structure of painting. As one might expect, Burki's cuts are not expressive iconoclastic gestures. The canvas is not slashed à la Lucio Fontana but is divided into discrete but proximate rectilinear sections in a careful, controlled, and planned manner. Burki also deconstructs both the frame around and the stretcher behind a traditional easel painting, reintroducing it into the picture plane through thin, mostly vertical, wooden slats or rods. These hybrid works function dialectically, not just by confounding Modernist medium specificity, but also by countering the rupture or the cut, a quintessential Modernist device, with, to continue the filmic metaphor, the fade. The fade is, of course, simply a gradation effect in film, a smoother, more gradual transition, as compared to the abruptness of the cut.

The first such work, *Minutes before I fall asleep*, 2019, [p. 90] is a simple segmented composition, a vertical rectangle divided into two separate sections, the top third painted white, the bottom two-thirds unpainted raw canvas. Where the two colours meet the canvas curls inwards like a roll of fabric or the end of a conveyer belt, as if the canvas simply wraps around and continues behind the picture plane. To draw attention to this subtle effect, Burki echoes the curve by flanking the canvas section with two wooden rods. The edge between the two segments is not sharp,

[12] Jacques Derrida, *The Truth in Painting*, trans. Geoff Bennington and Ian McLeod (Chicago: University of Chicago Press, 1987).

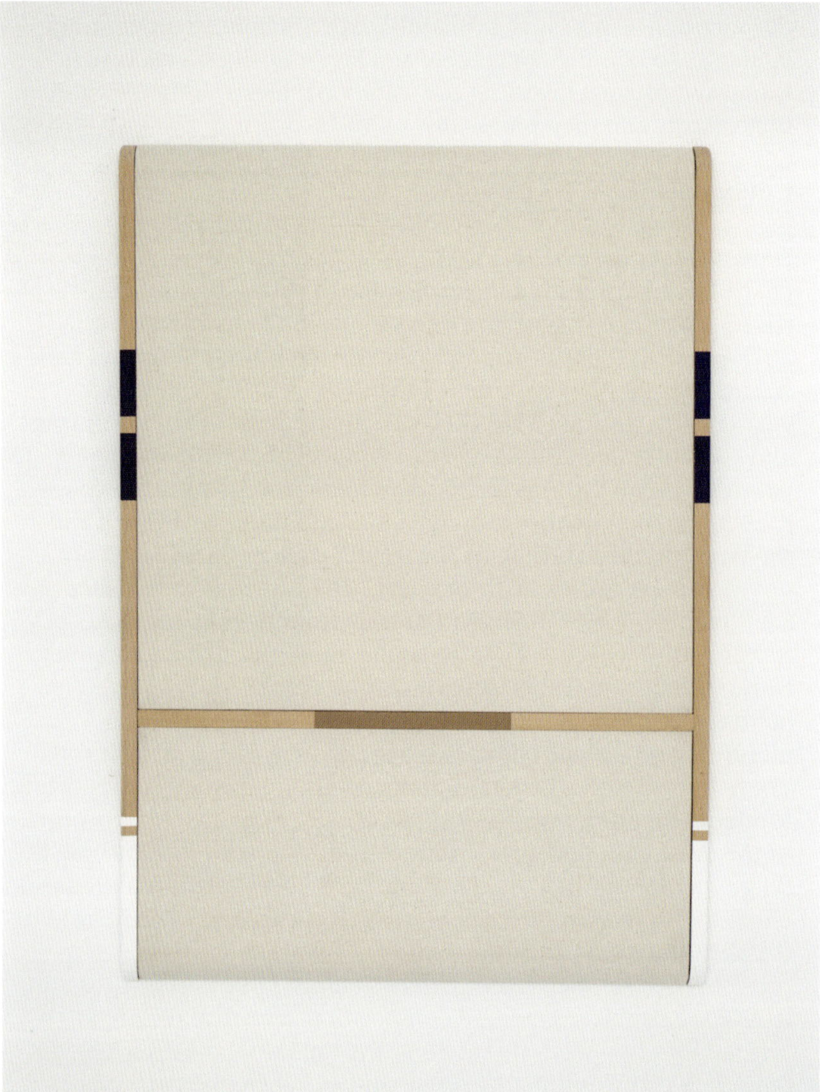

A tribe of one's own, 2020, wood, canvas, acrylic paint, 101.2 × 72.2 × 4.1 cm

it is not a cut but a fade. It does not represent division or separation but an encounter. It leaves wiggle room, allows space to breathe, is a grey area. It is a space of negotiation, of dialogue. *A tribe of one's own*, 2020, [p. 92] has a similar but inverted structure, so that the square appears above and the rectangle below. Both sections are left unpainted. Here the edge between the two is sharp, hardened by the inclusion of a horizontal wooden slat where the two canvases meet, creating a thin H-shaped wooden armature. Instead, it is the top and bottom edges of the painting that fade, that are rounded, softening the boundary between the painting and the wall behind it, so that the painting does not simply hang against the wall but curves into it, hugging it.

Burki further explored this contrast between sharp and rounded edges, between the cut and the fade, in a series of related coloured-pencil drawings from the same year. *Pencil Drawing III*, 2020, [p. 94] consists of four bands of different heights that alternate between heather grey and off-white. Burki uses gradation along each vertical edge to imply volume but varies the shape of the corners of each section; while those on the grey sections are mostly orthogonal, the ones on the off-white sections are rounded. It is a subtle detail that transforms the way the gradient effect functions spatially. The grey reads as surface, the off-white as volume. The former suggests cylinder, the latter torus. In *Pencil Drawing IV*, 2020, [p. 95] the rectangular field is divided horizontally into three differently coloured sections of varying heights. While the right edge of the rectangle darkens gradually, suggesting a curve into the paper, Burki uses a similar density of mark and colour to fill in a right-angle triangle on the left side that appears flush against the picture plane. Like so much of Burki's work, the drawing confounds, using the same chromatic and tonal values to convey both flatness and depth, both abstraction and illusion, within the same image.

Unframing

In *Minutes before I fall asleep* and *A tribe of one's own*, Burki has the wooden slats run the entire height of the canvas, serving as a bracket of sorts for the visual field within, complementing its simple symmetry. In others works from this series, they appear as fragments, incorporated within more complex if no less balanced compositions. As such, these works retain the possibility of internal tension, of scrambling the conventional logic of centre and periphery, picture

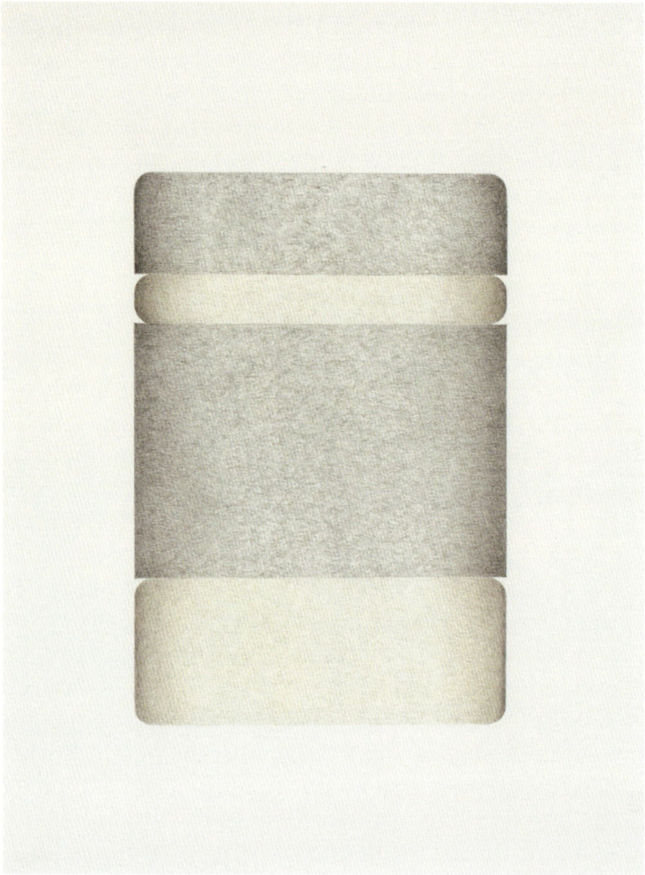

Pencil Drawing III, 2020, coloured pencil on paper, 50.3 × 37.7 cm

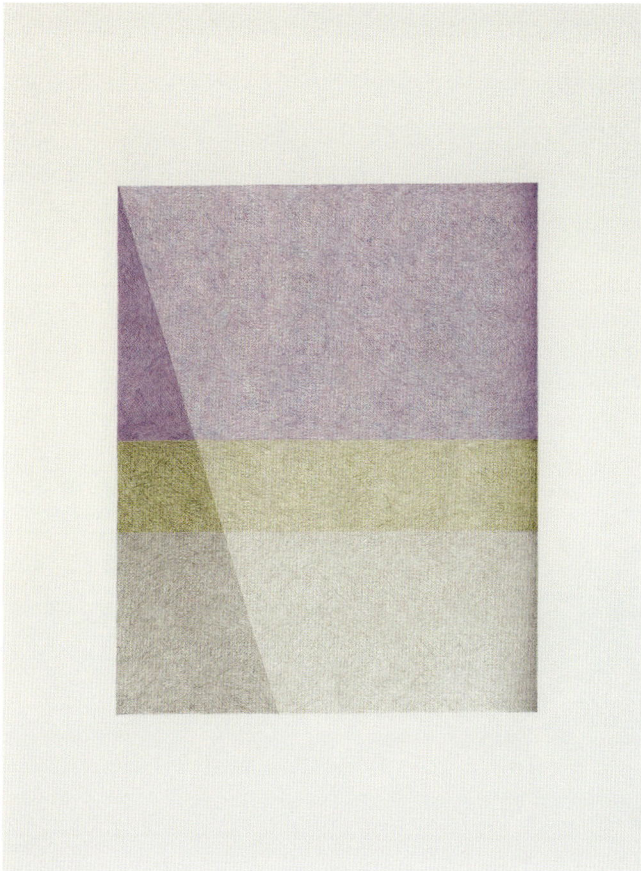

Pencil Drawing IV, 2020, coloured pencil on paper, 50.2 × 37.5 cm

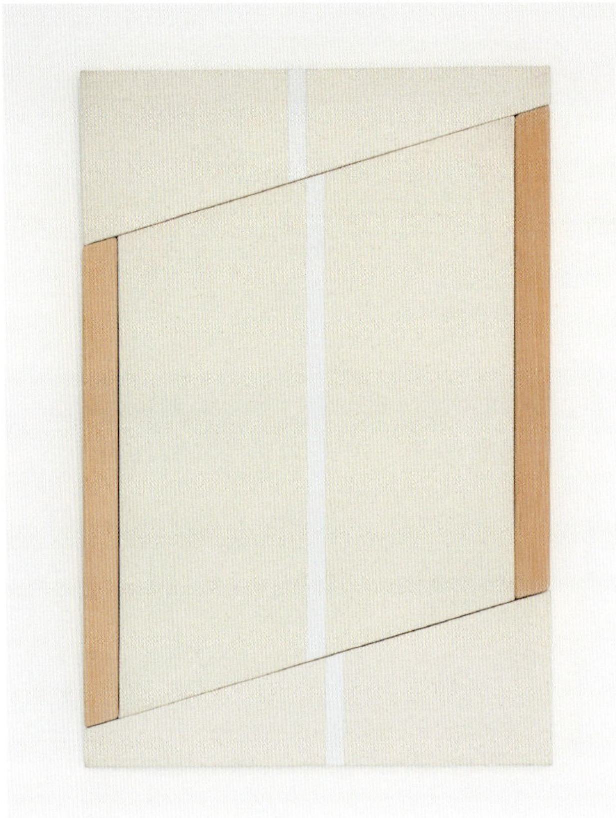

Parallels, 2020, wood, canvas, acrylic paint, 76.2 × 53.2 × 4.1 cm

and frame. Take *Parallels*, 2020, [p. 96] in which two wooden slats form the vertical sides of a parallelogram that is inset within the larger rectangular field, leaving a pair of almost triangular segments of canvas above and below it. Compressing the width of the visual field between them, these slats, along with the diagonal cuts that constitute the other two sides of the parallelogram, create tension within the frame, a displacement or torque, however, that remains internal to the picture, that does not threaten to break free. Burki dramatises this optical effect through the addition of a segmented pale-blue vertical line, which jumps to the right by its own thickness across each cut.

In a return to the square format he had previously used in 2015, *Idle Contemplation I* and *II*, both 2021, [pp. 98-99] are essentially deconstructed monochromes, composites of variously sized squares and rectangles of unpainted canvas, some of which are flanked on one side by wooden slats. Occasionally, two slats partially overlap, momentarily thickening the edge. In *Idle Contemplation II*, the wooden fragments remain at the perimeter, suggesting an incomplete outline, a broken frame. In *Idle Contemplation I*, they break into the picture plane – like the orbs embedded in Jasper Johns's iconic *Painting with Two Balls*, 1960 – the frame displaced from the periphery towards the centre. The edges of these composites are intentionally left uneven and incomplete, so that we are never able to default to our conventional understanding of what might constitute a frame or a canvas. By shattering the unity and continuity of both canvas and frame, Burki blurs the distinction between them. We are unframed but made to remain on edge. Contemplating these objects is hardly an idle pursuit.

Narrative, Again

Despite the conceptual rigour of works like *Idle Contemplation I* and *II*, subject matter, narrative, and metaphor are slowly but surely creeping back into Burki's practice. Take *Amaryllis*, 2020, [p. 102] whose tripartite structure – a large canvas square, its left edge lined with a piece of wood, sitting atop two rectangular canvases of equal height and unequal width – is embellished with two leaf-like slivers of pale green. Extending into the centre from the lower left corner of the square and the lower right corner of the smaller rectangle, these details balance the irregular structure of the visual field. But they also evoke the titular plant, and a time, a place, a sensation, a memory. Or *Beach*, 2021, [p. 103] with its

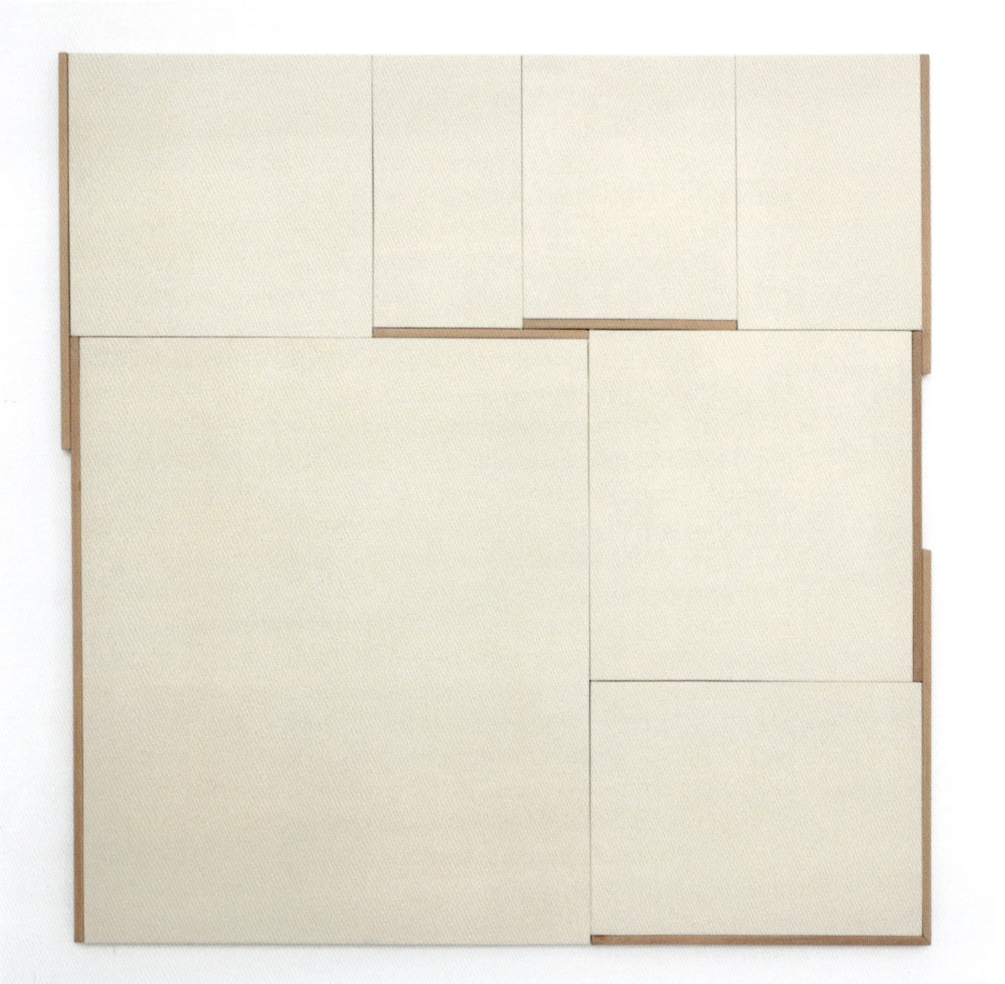

Idle Contemplation I, 2021, acrylic, canvas and wood, 183 × 183 × 6 cm

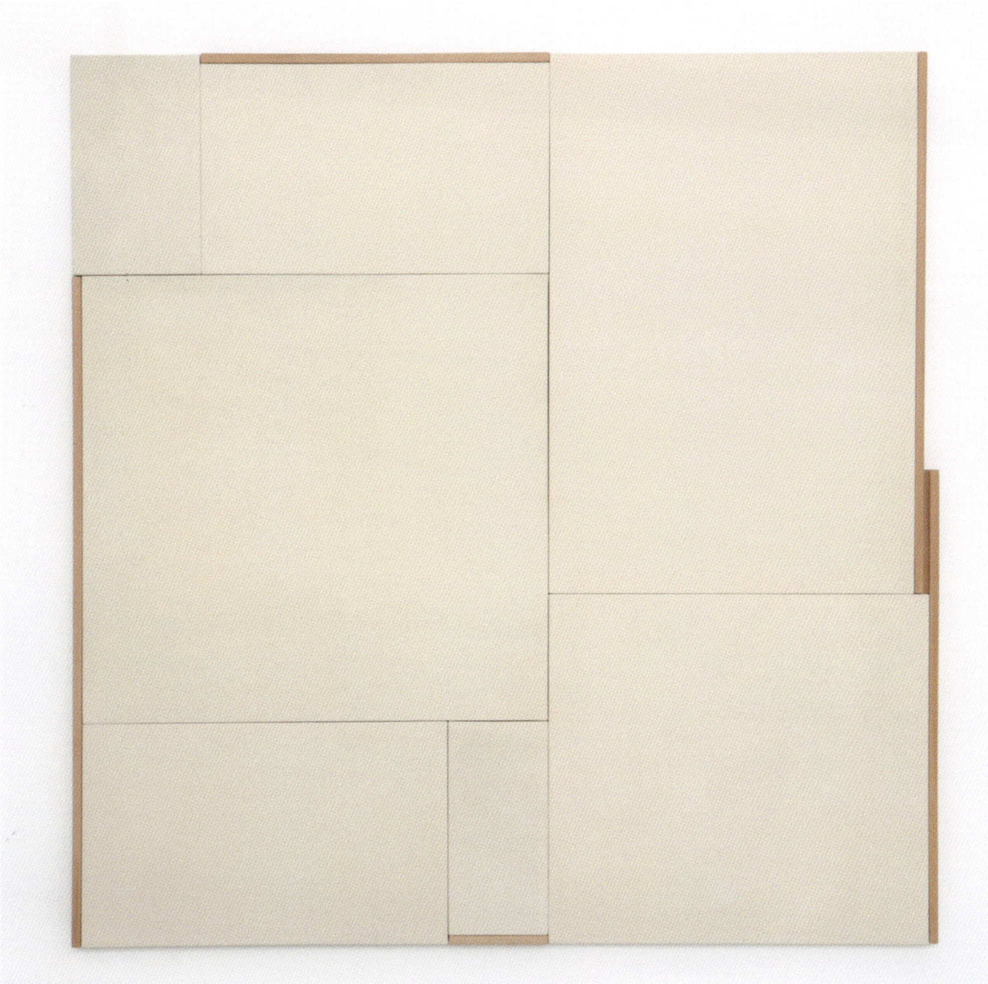

Idle Contemplation II, 2021, acrylic, canvas and wood, 183 × 183 × 6 cm

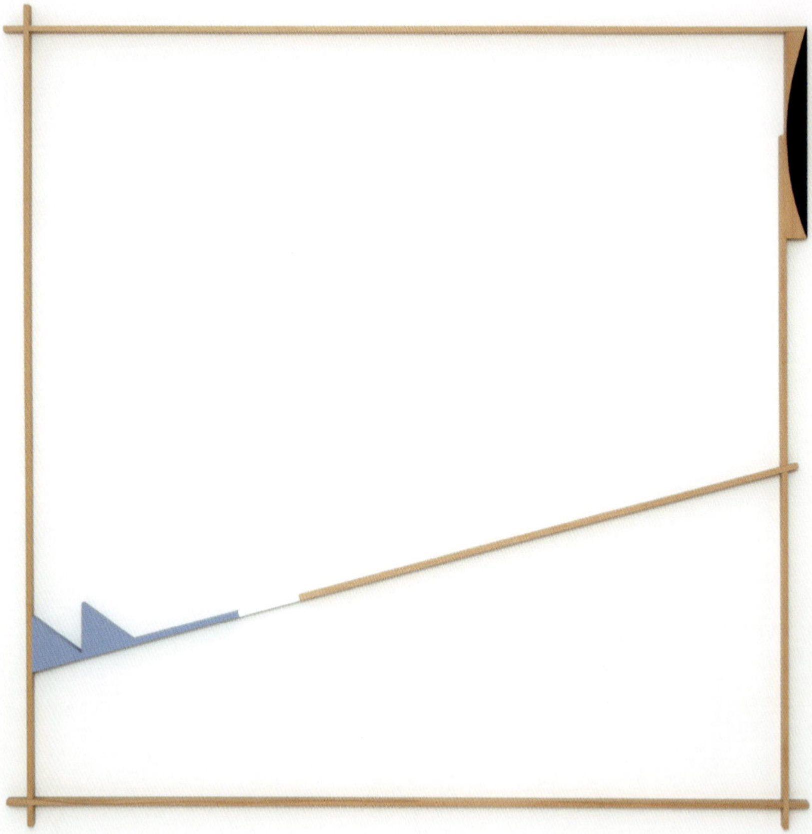

Archer, 2021, acrylic on beechwood, 152.5 × 152.5 × 4 cm

palette of *Miami Vice* pastels, its almost too-literal sandy ground, and its pair of undulating parallel lines, a white one shadowed by a light-grey one, the displacement between them succinctly evoking both time and space. The lines suggest the water's edge or the presence of the overhead sun. Or *Archer*, 2021, [p. 100] which, like *Affinity*, 2020, [p. 104] and *Dwelling* (grey), 2020, [p. 105] forgoes canvas entirely for an all-wood construction. However, *Archer* goes a step further, forgoing a surface for paint or picture entirely. Delineated by four thin wooden slats, the square field remains empty. A thin diagonal piece of wood bisects the field, two light-blue triangles attached to its left end transforming it into an arrow. A sliver of a black circle fills a slightly thicker wooden fragment attached to the top right corner, suggesting a bow. *Archer* is all frame, all stretcher, all structure. Centre and periphery, frame and surface, figuration and abstraction, are everywhere and nowhere, all at once.

In *Archer*, the ability of artwork to interrogate the structures of abstraction and to tell stories no longer appears oppositional or mutually exclusive. Burki's experiments in minimal abstraction over the last decade represent a sustained process through which its restrained, refined and at times literal idiom has been opened up gradually – through the fade and other strategies – to complex spatial and temporal effects, and to the possibilities and potentialities of narrative and metaphor. In retrospect, Burki's minimalism reveals itself as an ongoing process, a working method, a slow fade, possibly back to the beginning, to stories, now whispered not told.

Beach, 2021, acrylic on canvas, 84 × 64 × 3 cm
(opposite) *Amaryllis*, 2020, wood, canvas, acrylic paint, 100.2 × 70 × 4.1 cm

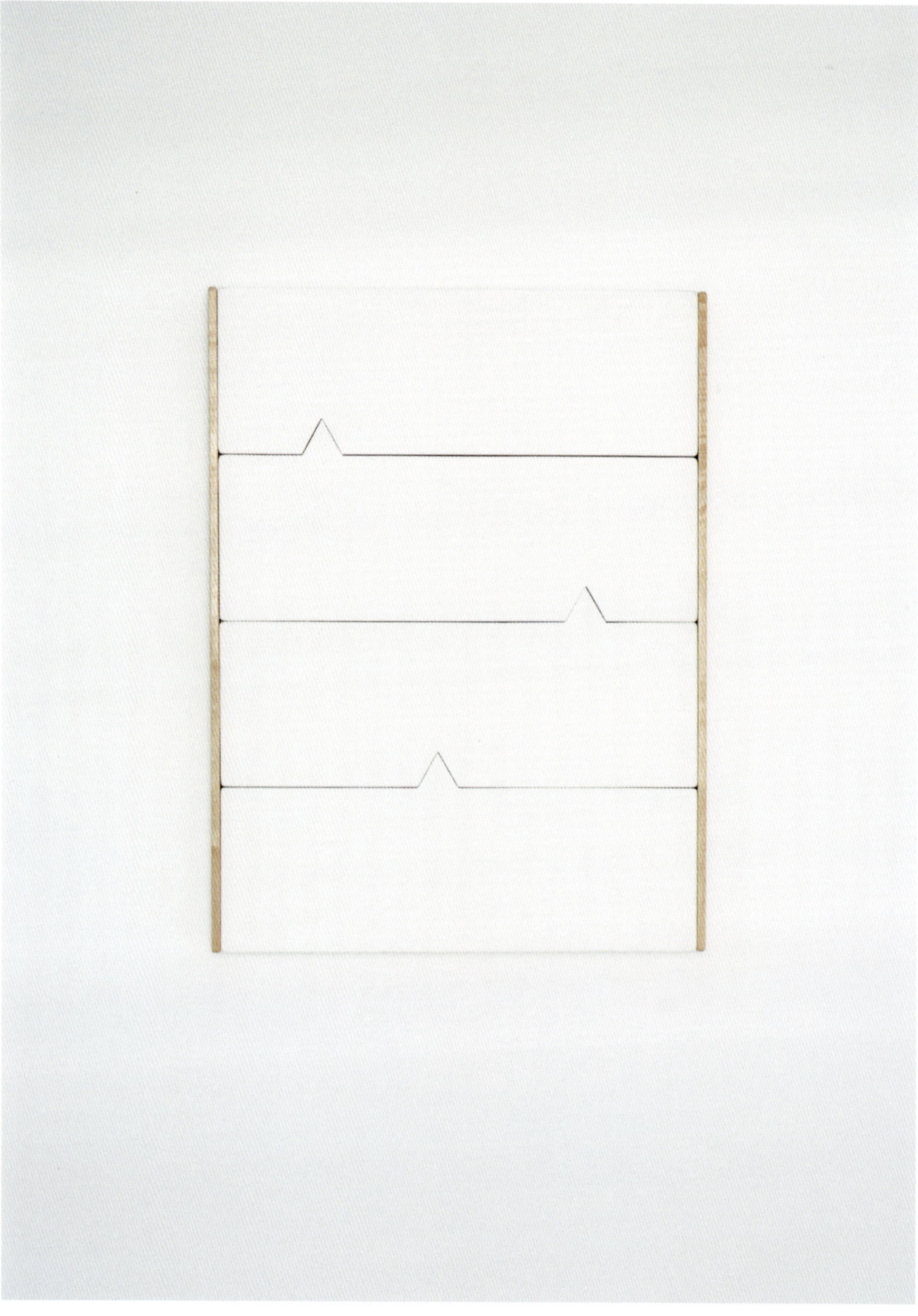

Affinity, 2020, wood, acrylic gesso, 75.4 × 58 × 4.1 cm

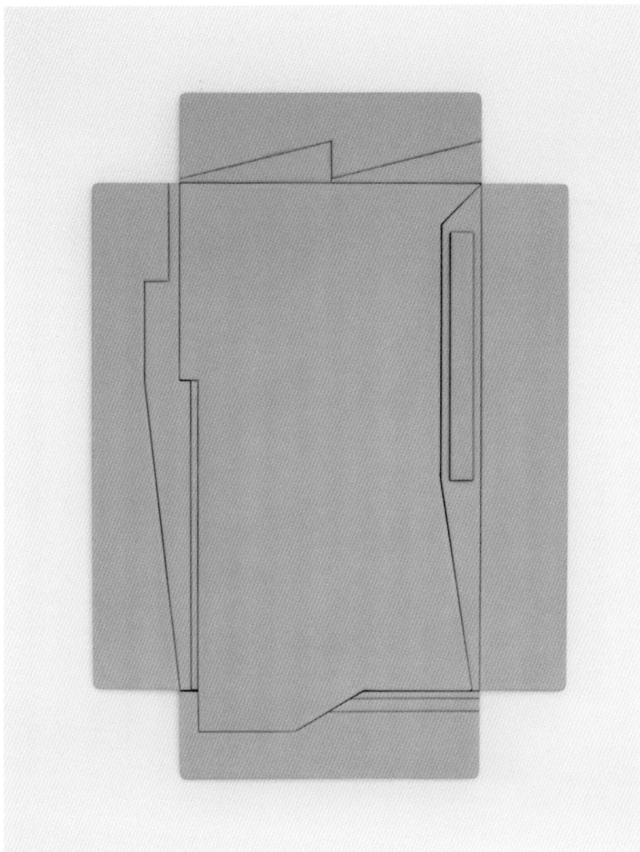

Dwelling (grey), 2020, wood, ply, acrylic paint, 90.7 × 64.4 × 4 cm

Meet, 2021, acrylics, canvas and wood, 105 × 69.7 × 4.2 cm

EXHIBITION VIEWS

Fahd Burki

daydreams

Curated by Dawn Ross

Jameel Arts Centre, Dubai

5 March – 9 October, 2022

Courtesy of Art Jameel. Photos by Daniella Baptista.

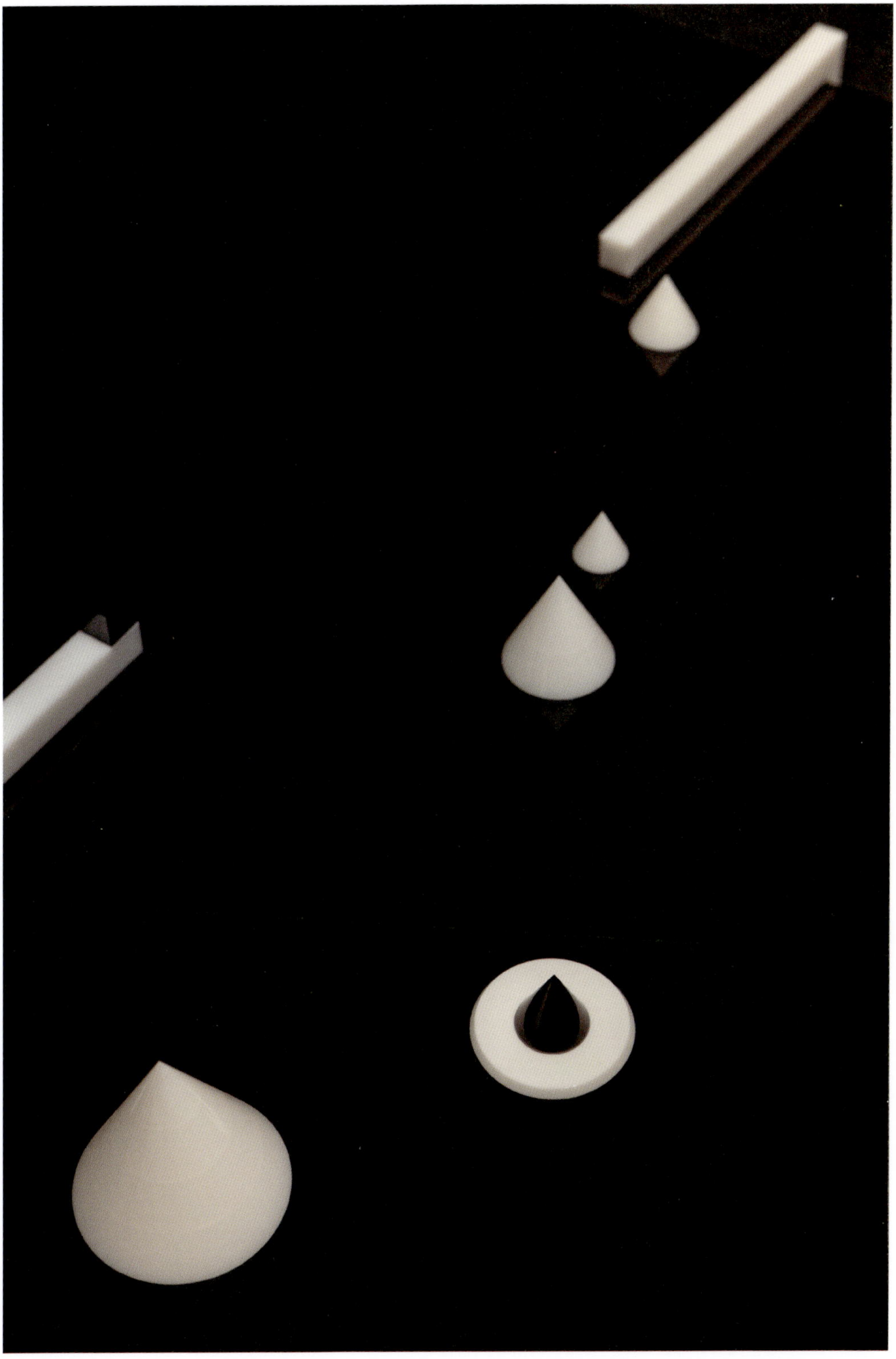

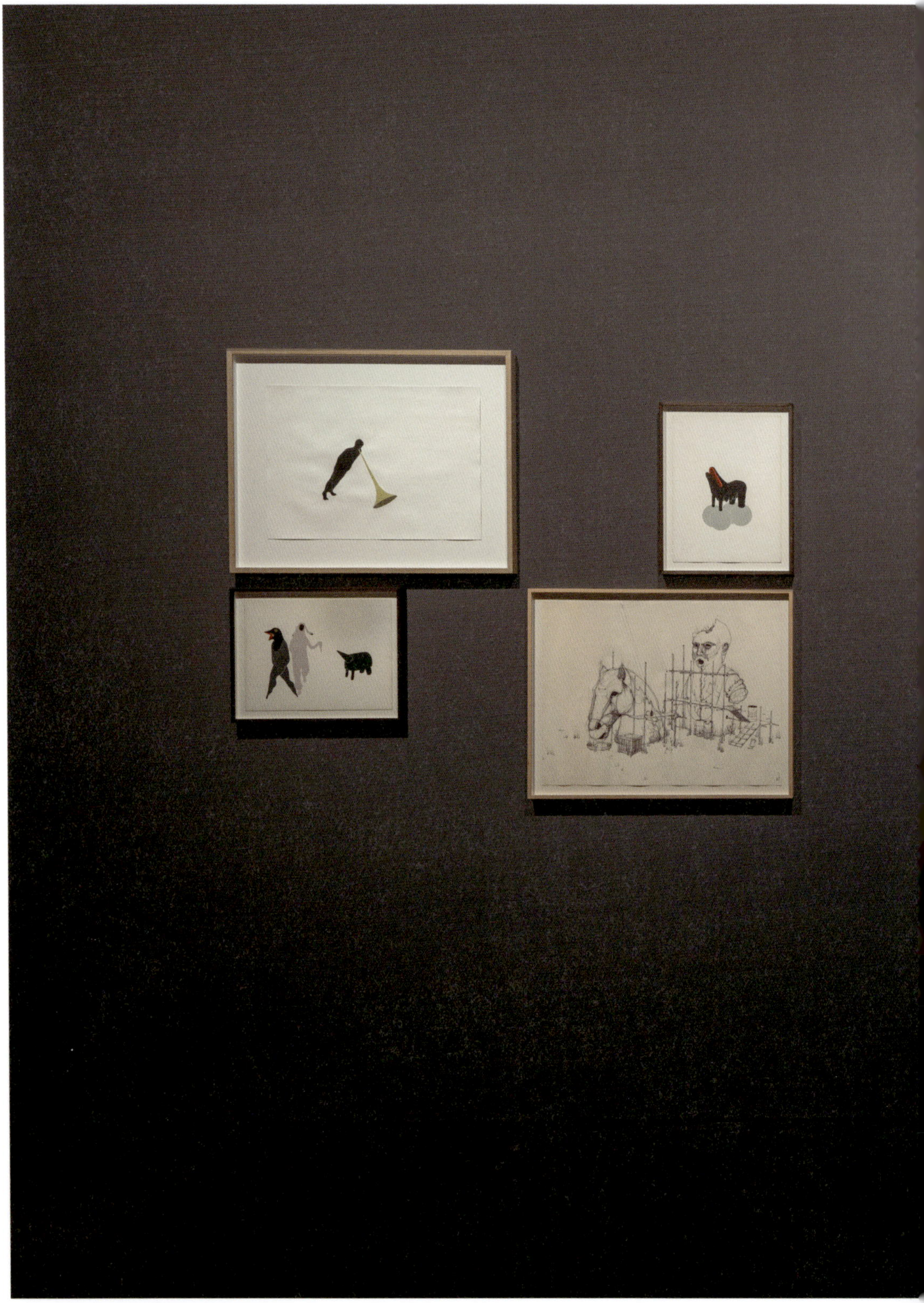

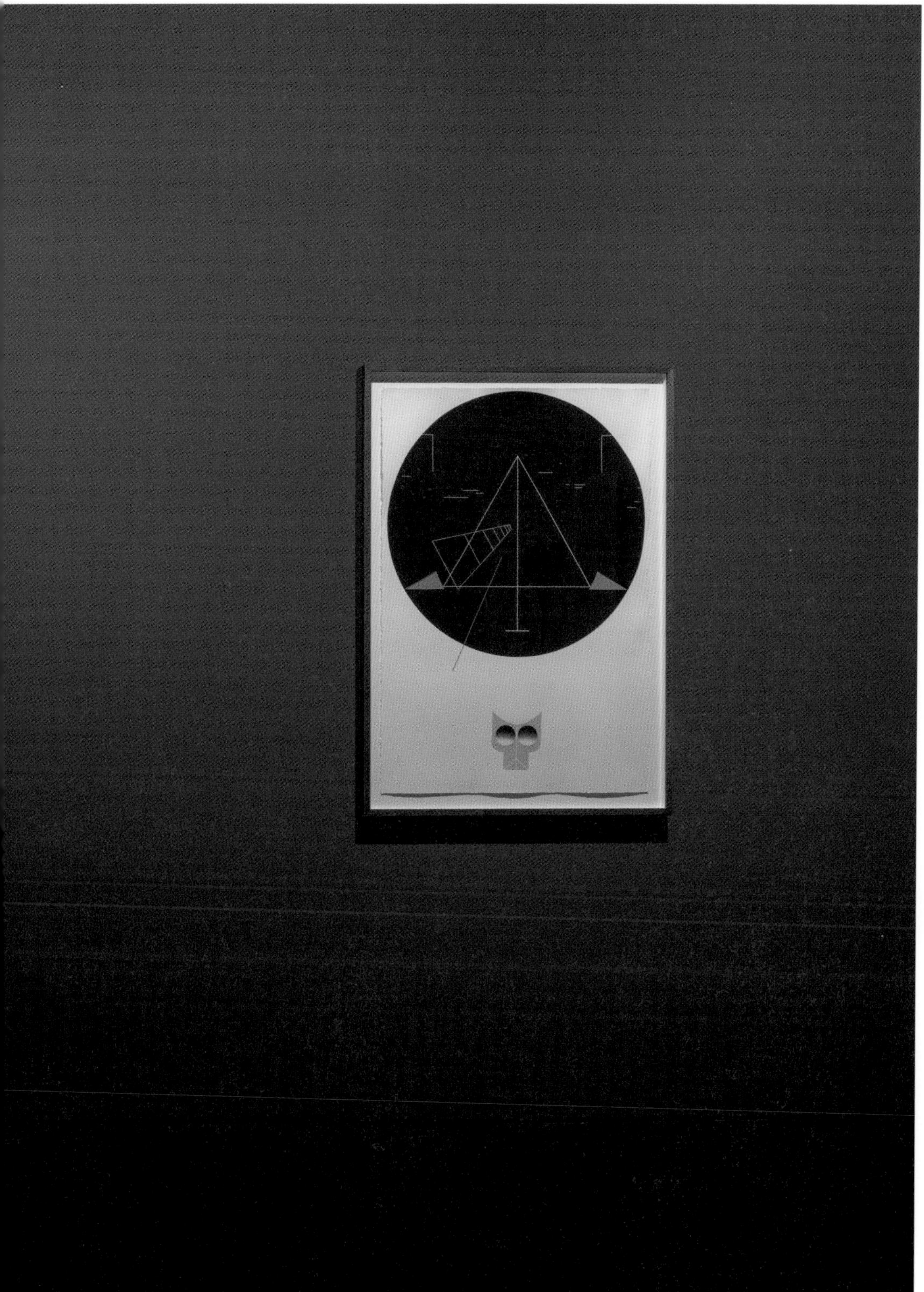

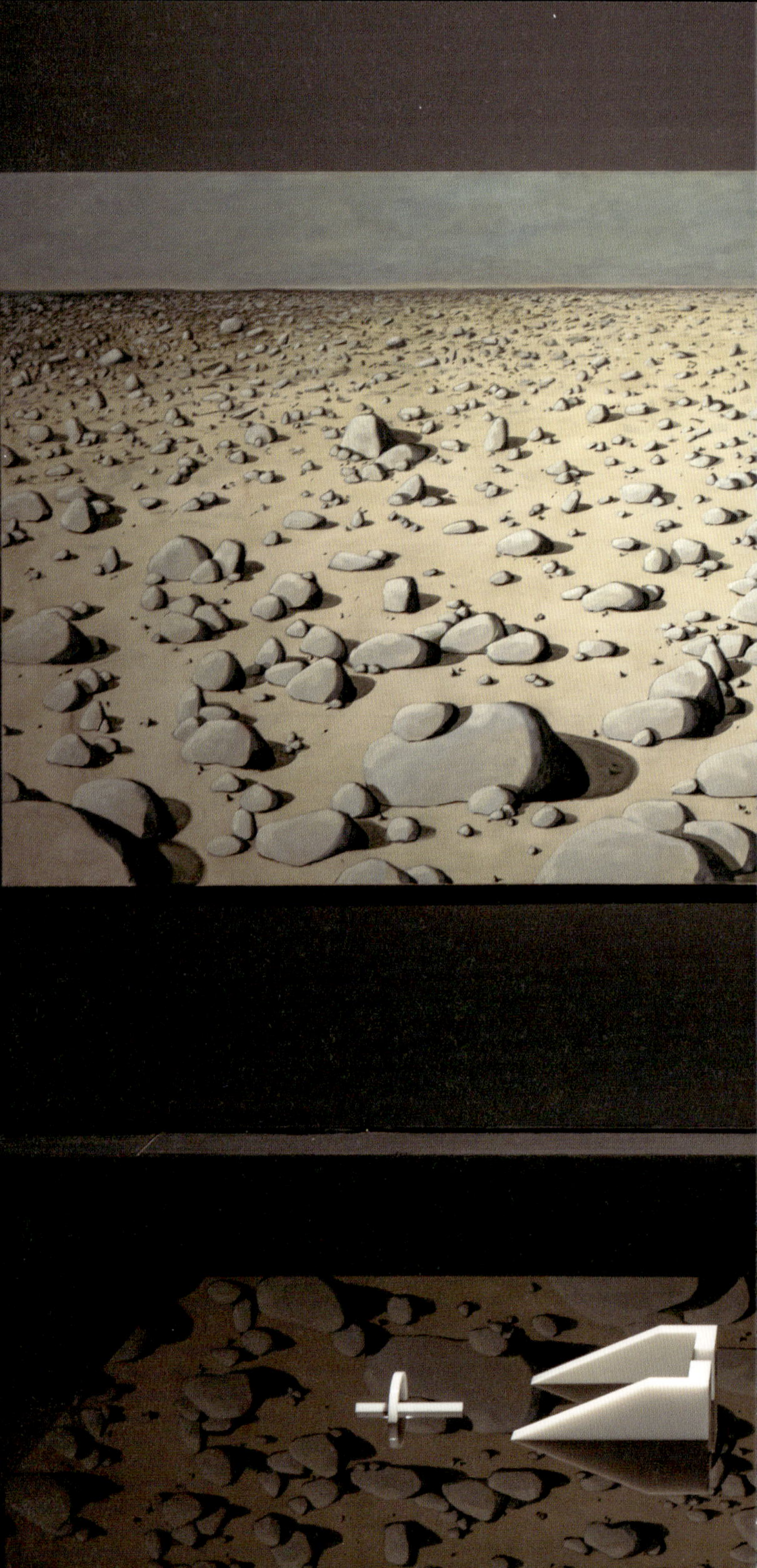

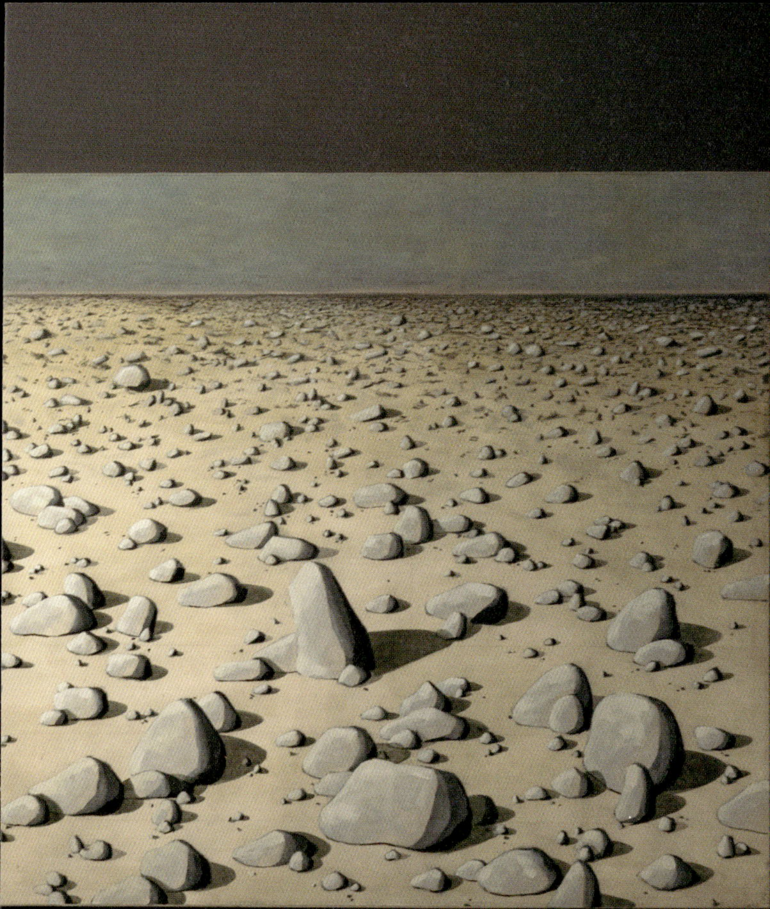

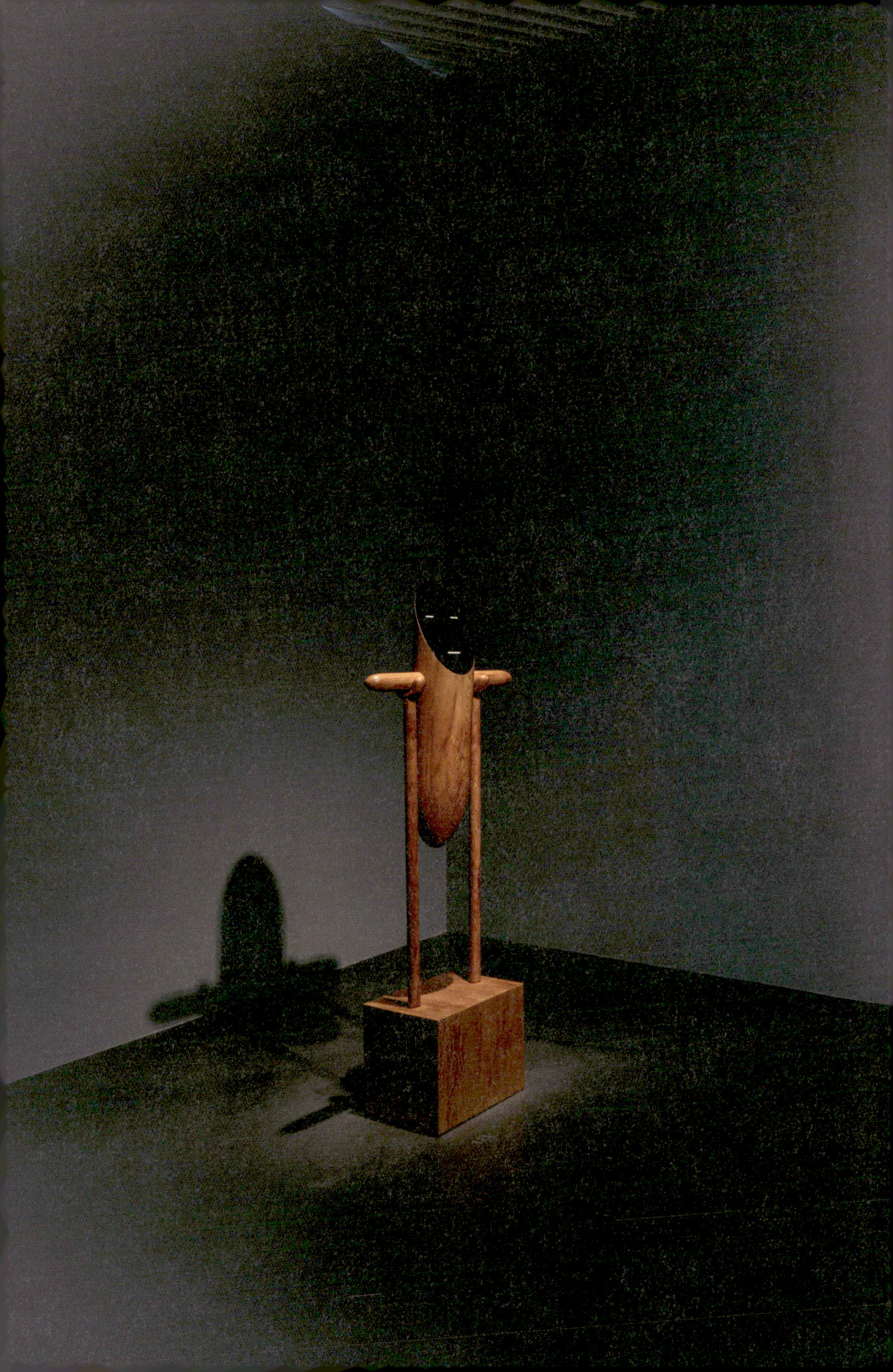

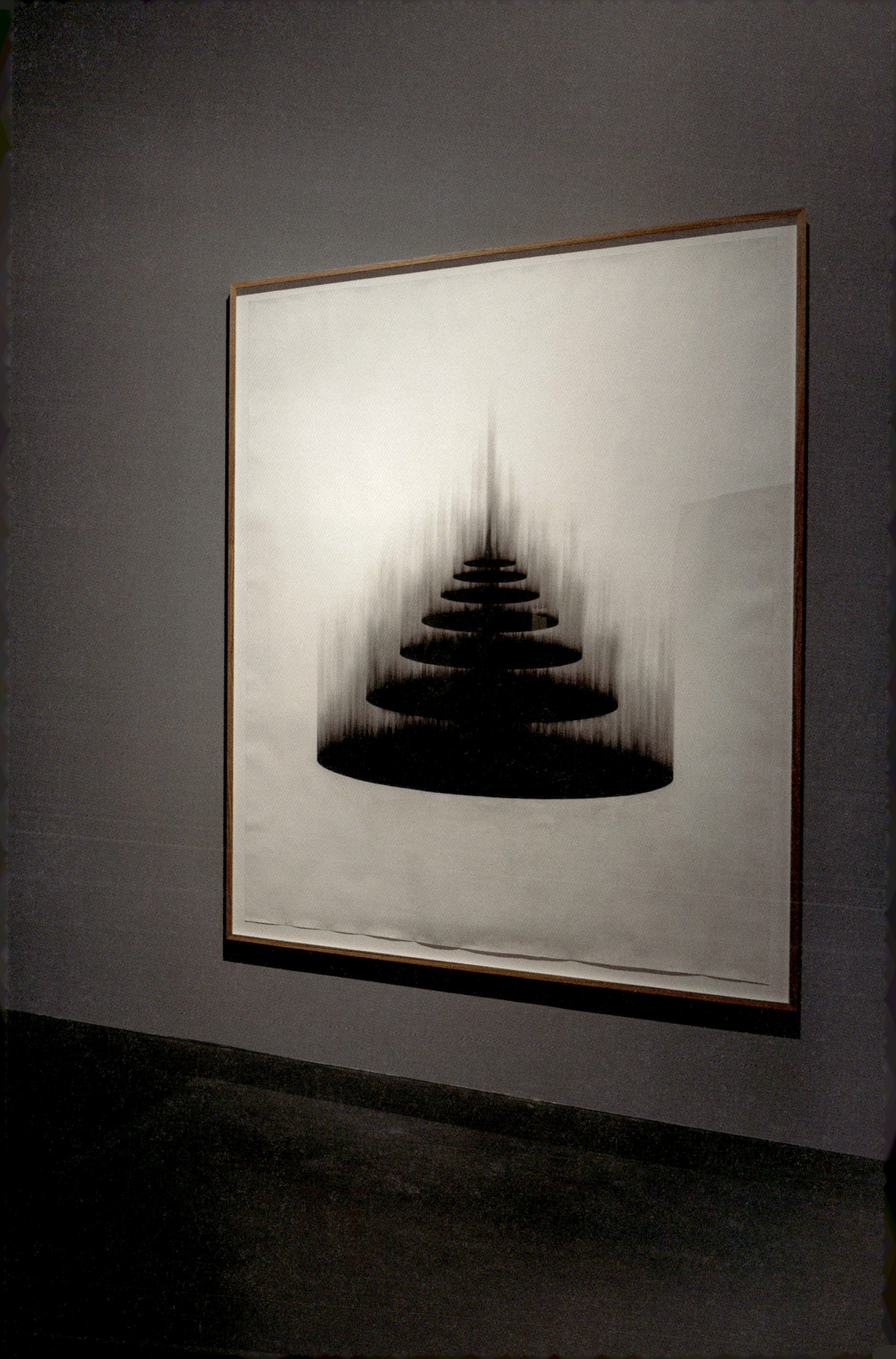

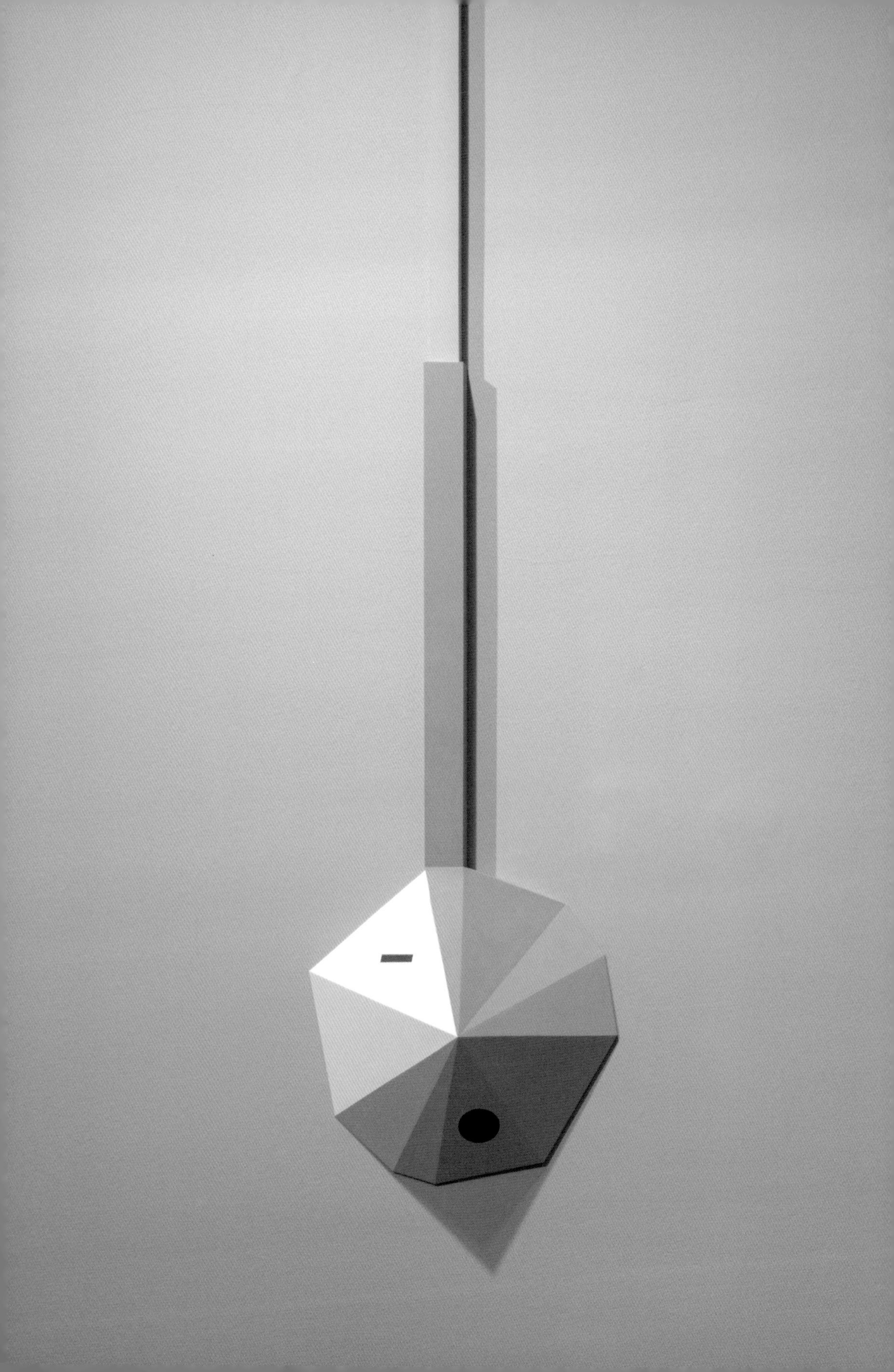

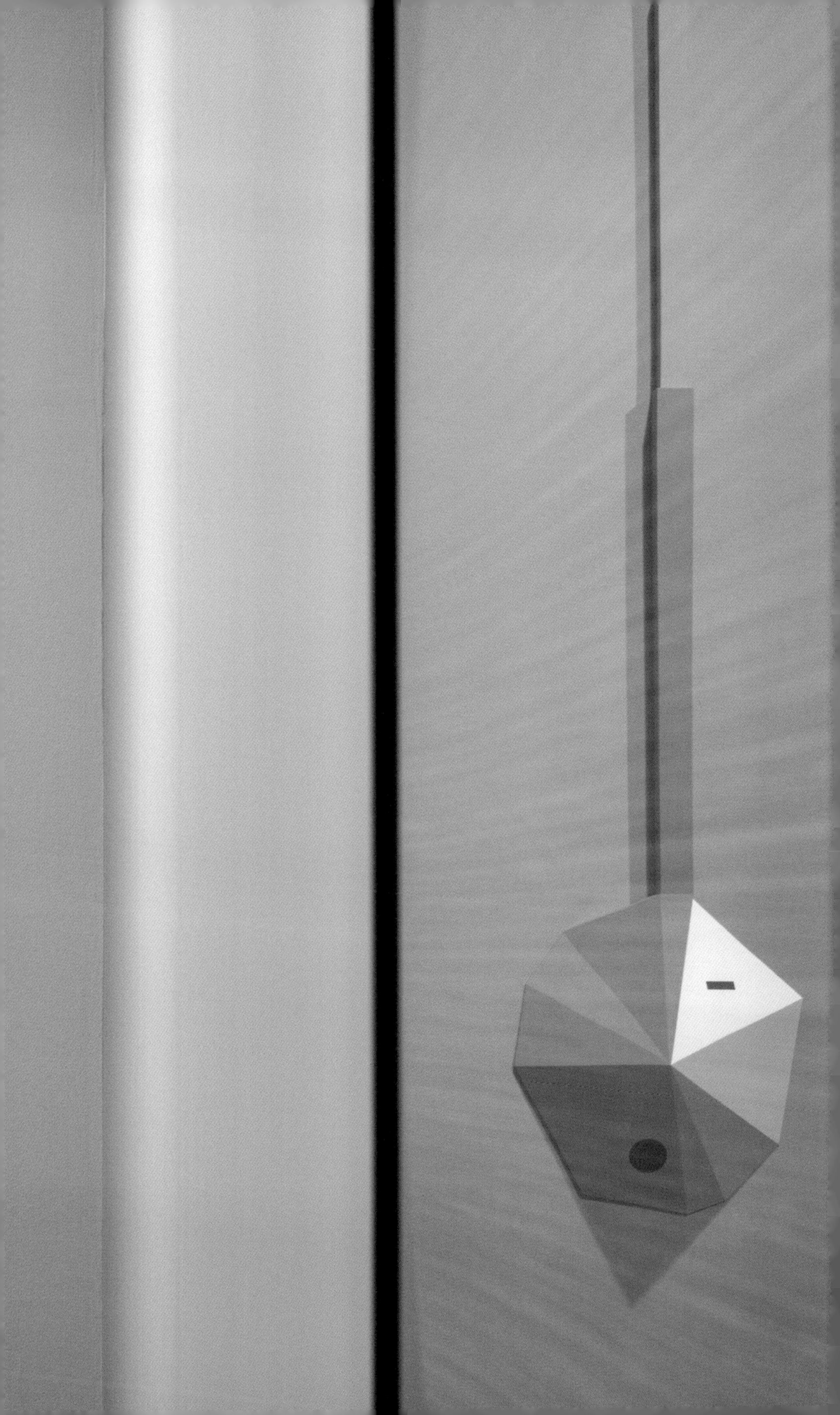

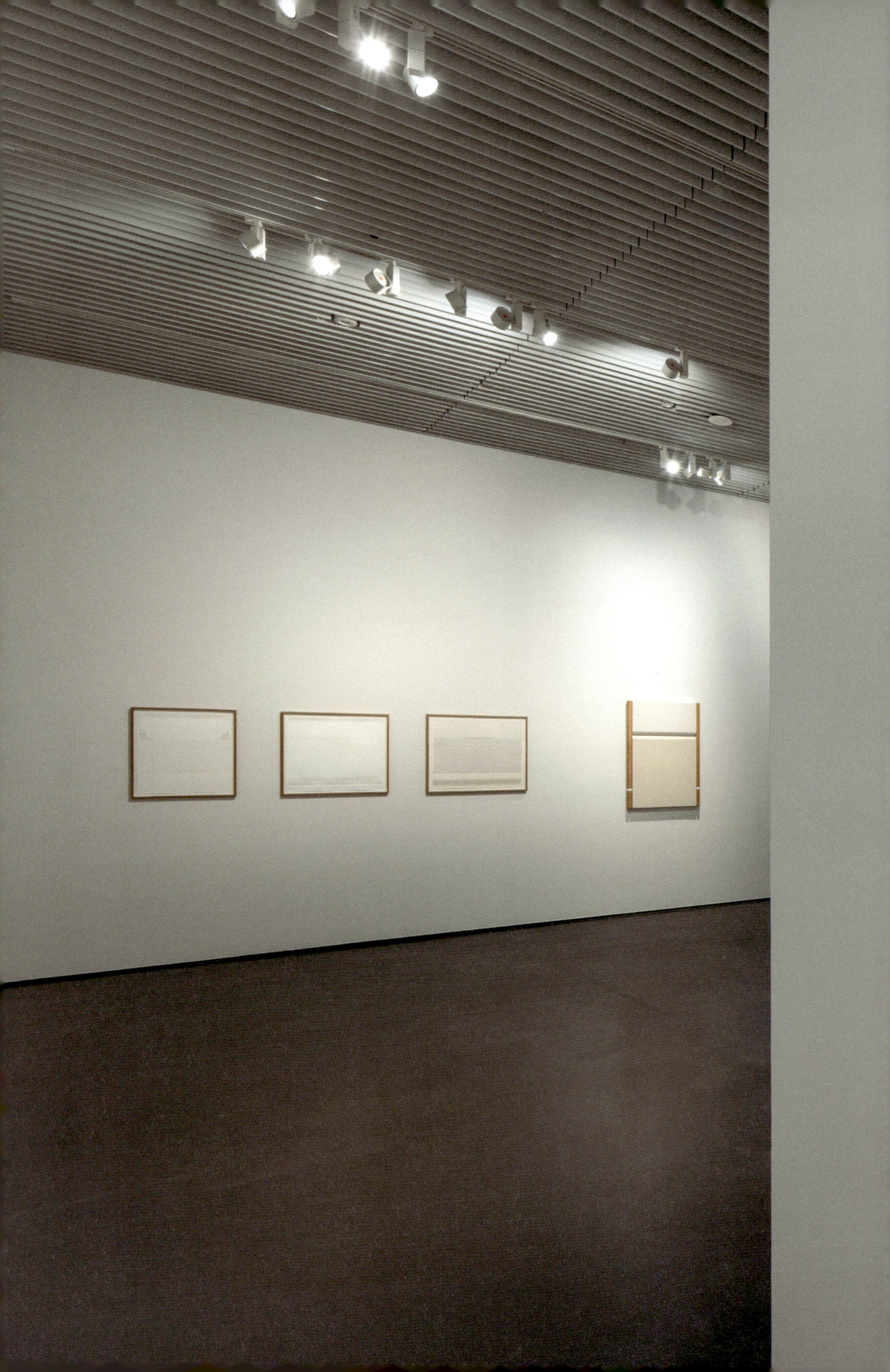

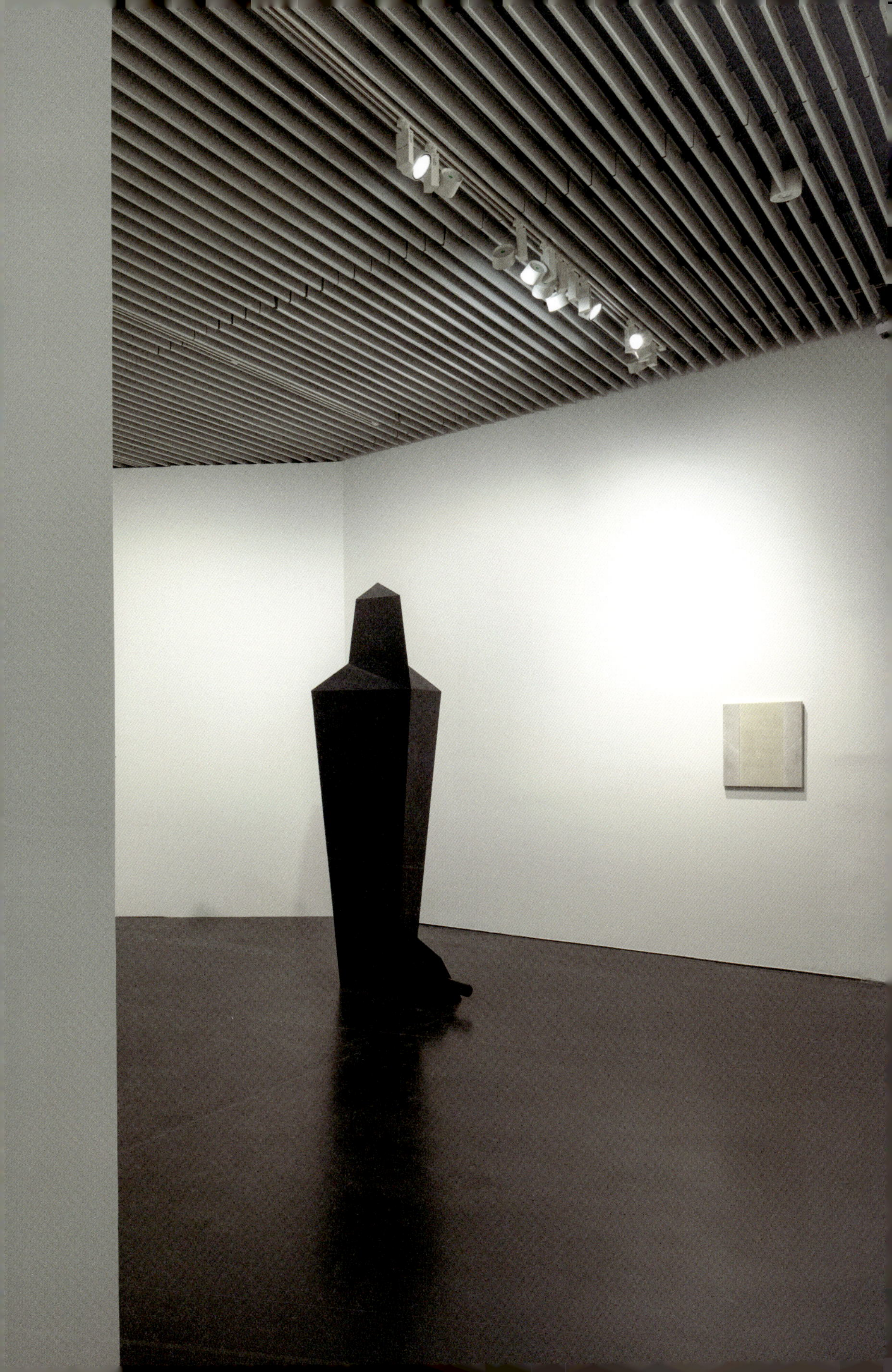

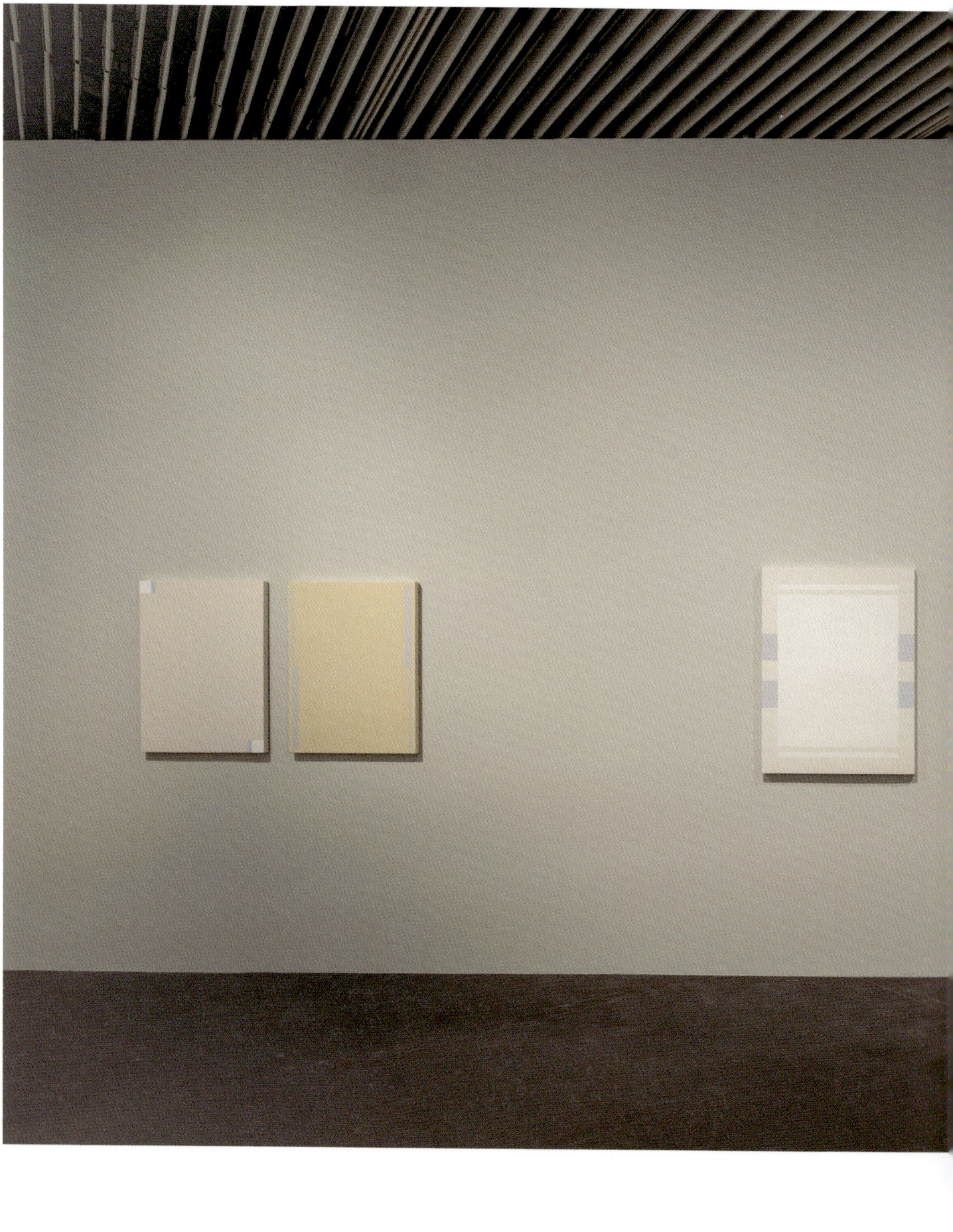

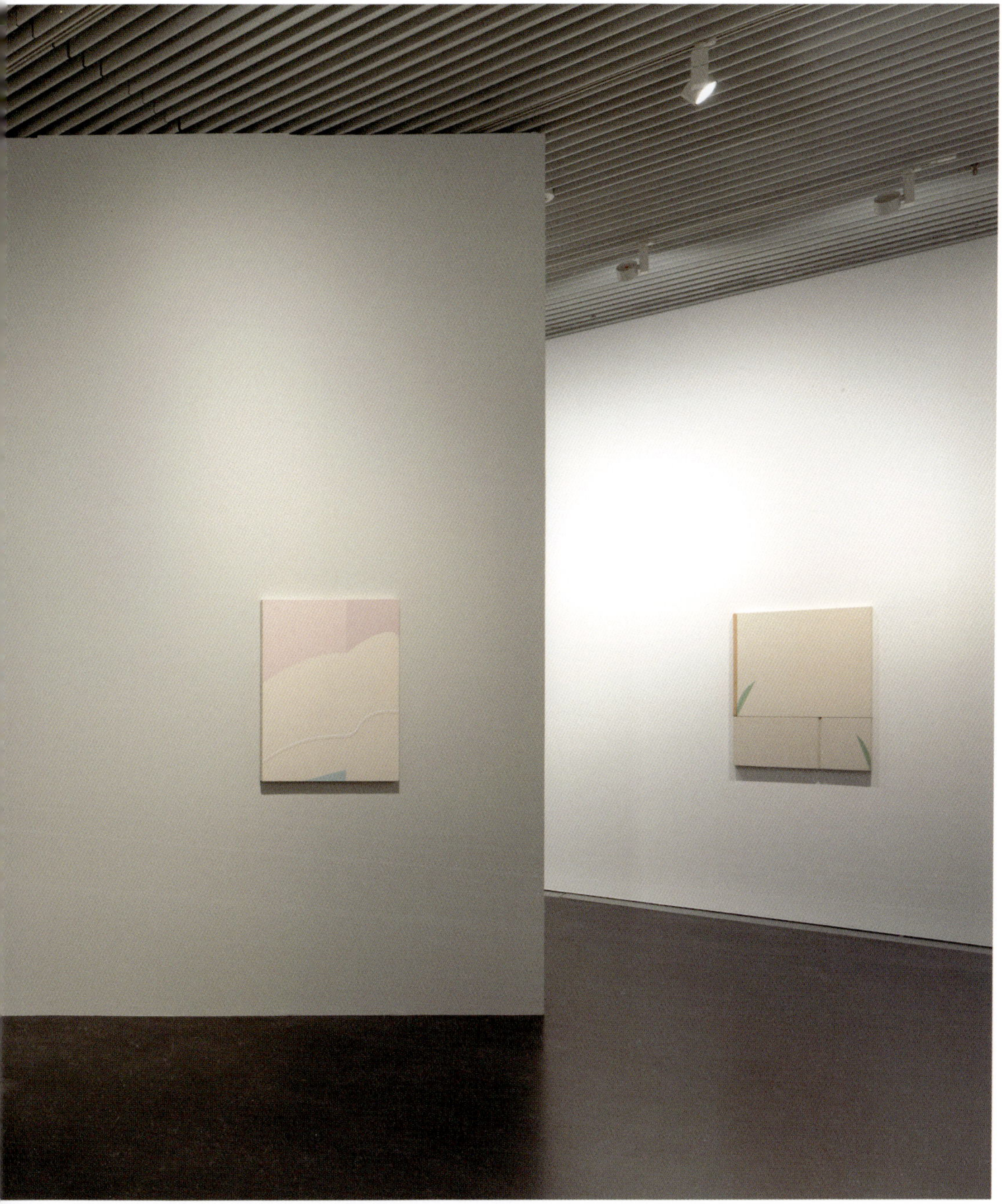

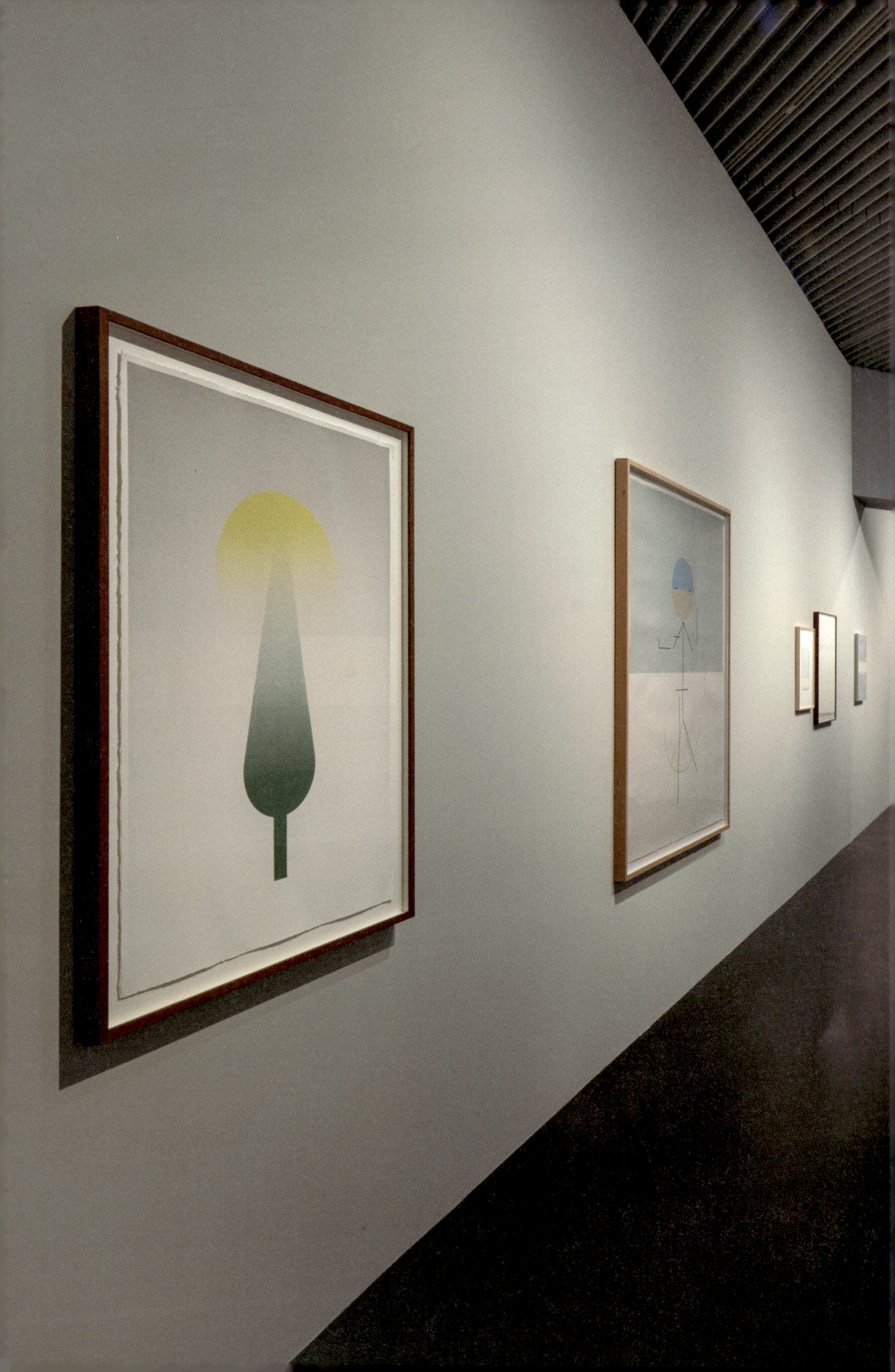

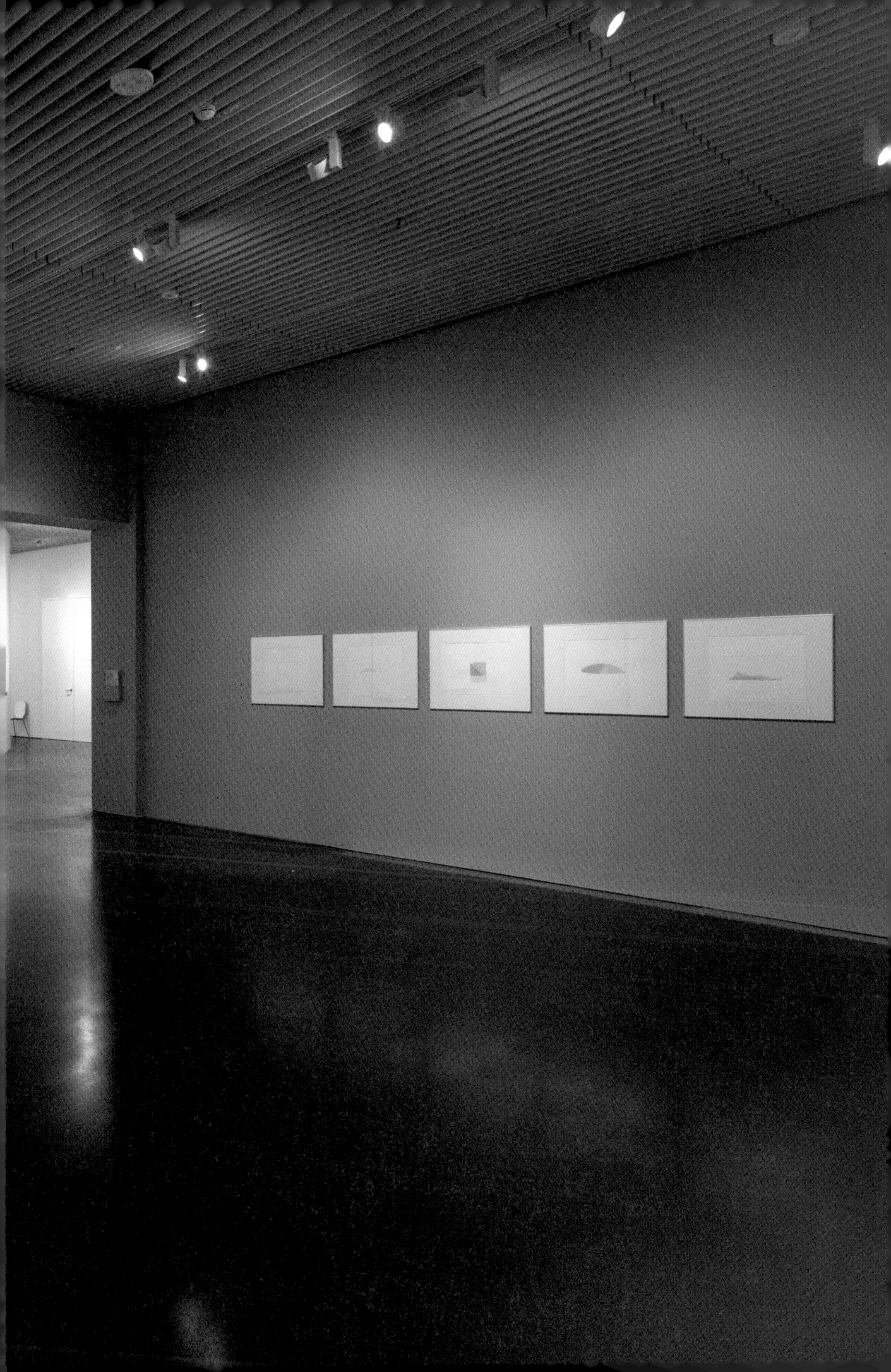

BIOGRAPHIES

Saira Ansari (lives and works in Dubai, United Arab Emirates) is an independent writer and researcher employing creative non-fiction to think about art practice and criticism, feminist histories, gardens, grief, science fiction, and South Asia and its real and imagined peripheries. As an editor, Ansari has worked with a wide range of artists and writers from across South Asia, the Middle East and Iran. Recent projects include the upcoming monographs on Bani Abidi (Hatje Cantz, 2022) and Sahand Hesamiyan (Black Dog Press, 2023). Previously, Ansari worked at Sharjah Art Foundation where she managed book projects and the FOCAL POINT art book fair. Ansari's research focuses also on Pakistani modernist Zubeida Agha and projects include the Zubeida Agha Archive hosted by Asia Art Archive, Hong Kong.

Fahd Burki (lives and works in Lahore, Pakistan) graduated from the National College of Arts, Lahore in 2003 and received a Postgraduate Diploma from the Royal Academy of Arts, London in 2010. His work has been exhibited widely in solo and group shows internationally, including Jameel Arts Centre, Dubai, 2022; 9th Göteborg International Biennial for Contemporary Art, 2017; National Gallery of Art, Warsaw, 2016; Gwangju Biennale 11, 2016; Office for Contemporary Art Norway: OCA, Oslo, 2016; Dhaka Art Summit, 2016; British Council Headquarters, London, 2015; and Carré d'Art, Nîmes, 2014. In 2014, a monograph of the artist's work was published in association with Skira, Milan.

Dawn Ross (lives and works in Dubai, United Arab Emirates) is Head of Collections at Art Jameel, overseeing the Art Jameel Collection and associated exhibitions – at Jameel Arts Centre, Dubai, and Hayy Jameel, Jeddah – and loans with partner museums regionally and internationally. Previously, she has worked in arts institutions and festivals in Australia, Scotland and the United Arab Emirates, most recently heading up not-for-profit artist's projects at Art Dubai.

Murtaza Vali (lives and works in Sharjah, United Arab Emirates; and Brooklyn, United States) is a critic, curator, and art historian. His ongoing research interests include materialist art histories, ex-centric minimalisms, ghosts and other figures of liminal subjectivities and repressed histories, the weight of colour and contemporary art of the Indian Ocean littoral. A recipient of the 2011 Creative Capital | Warhol Foundation Arts Writers Grant for Short-Form Writing, he publishes regularly in various international art periodicals and in exhibition catalogues for not-for-profit institutions and commercial galleries worldwide. Vali is Curator-at-large of FRONT International 2022: Cleveland Triennial for Contemporary Art and Adjunct Curator at the Jameel Arts Centre, Dubai, where he curated the widely acclaimed inaugural group exhibition *Crude* (2018), which explored the relationship between oil and modernity across South West Asia.